Edinburgh Memories
And Some Worthies

BY

J. WILSON M'LAREN

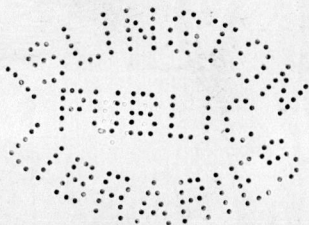

LONDON: 38 Soho Square, W.1

W. & R. CHAMBERS, LIMITED

EDINBURGH: 339 High Street

1926

Printed in Great Britain.
W. & R. CHAMBERS, LTD., LONDON and EDINBURGH.

TO THE EARL OF ROSEBERY,
A SCOT OF SCOTS, AND
LOVER OF OLD EDINBURGH,
THIS BOOK IS INSCRIBED
WITHOUT PERMISSION . . .

Extract from a letter of Robert Louis Stevenson's to the Author.

'Cocoa-nut Tam, though it argue me unknown myself, I do not seem to be able to place, unless he were an honest merchant at the head of the Lawn Market!'

E.M.—*Front.*

FOREWORD.

THE following sketches deal mainly with the life of an Edinburgh generation that is fast passing away. They are the outcome of the author's own experience and observation during a lifetime spent in the city, and contain memories of men and affairs that cannot be found elsewhere. Born and reared within the ancient Royalty, the writer had special opportunities of becoming familiar with notable persons during the changeful years of the 'seventies and 'eighties, and of taking part in incidents of that interesting period when the city was beginning to evolve into the Greater Edinburgh of the present.

The study of current events in Edinburgh in the seventh and eighth decades of the nineteenth century, and of the earlier history and associations of the Old Town, was the writer's favourite recreation. He mixed with 'characters' of the town, and gathered many stories from them. From the older inhabitants, also, he collected much interesting material. These gleanings are incorporated in the following pages.

During the past half-century the writer has taken an active interest, and sometimes a prominent part, in the many movements—civic, social, literary, and re-creative—which have marked the development of the

7

city. He thus became acquainted, and remained on terms of friendship, with the most distinguished sons of the city and those who have become identified with it. Memories of these, and particularly of his meetings and correspondence with Robert Louis Stevenson, Sir Henry Irving, Andrew Lang, and others, are included in the sketches.

Many requests from lovers of Old Edinburgh, in every part of the habitable globe, have induced the writer to issue these Memories in a more permanent, and somewhat extended form, in the hope that it may save them from being relegated to the limbo of things forgotten.

The articles in this volume have appeared in the *Scotsman*, *Weekly Scotsman*, *Edinburgh Evening Dispatch*, *Edinburgh Evening News*, and *Scots Pictorial*. The author thanks the Proprietors for kind permission to reprint them.

CONTENTS

LIST OF ILLUSTRATIONS

13

BY THE SAME AUTHOR.

SCOTS POEMS AND BALLANTS.
TIBBIE AND TAM.
JOHN o' HOWGATE.
WEIR THE WIZARD.
A SAINTLY SINNER.
A CANNY SCOT.

PLAYS.

WEIR OF HERMISTON.
OVER THE SEA TO SKYE.

Edinburgh Memories
And Some Worthies.

THE ROYAL MILE.

IN what patriotic Scot's memory do not
recollections linger of a visit to the High
Street and Canongate, and the relics of the
past? At 'hame or ower the sea' he can
still vividly recall the 'Heave Awa'' land,
and John Knox's House at the Netherbow;
and, farther down, the balcony of Moray
House, from which, on 18th May 1650, the
Marquis of Montrose was spat on by the
Marchioness of Argyll on his way to prison
—and death. Huntly House, that picturesque 'bit,' which has been acquired by the
Corporation, and, on the opposite side, the
Old Tolbooth, with its quaint cross, are also
familiar.

At the 'Mercat Croce' announcements of
peace and war, of national rejoicing and
national grief, were made. Here Stuart
kings and their successors were proclaimed

as monarchs; Oliver Cromwell, and afterwards his son, were proclaimed Protectors.
Many stirring scenes connected with Bonnie
Prince Charlie and the '45 were enacted at
the 'Mercat Croce.' Here, too, John Knox,
the great Scottish Reformer, was burned—in

Moray House.

effigy. And many others were burned—not
in effigy! Under this relic of bygone days
stood the 'branks,' the pillory, the 'maiden,'
and the gallows, and punishment was inflicted
which more than met the crime. At the
High Street 'Croce' bankrupts had to show

themselves to the citizens, seated, 'with caps and dress half brown and half yellow, from 10 A.M. till one hour after dinner'!

To-day, the shaft of the old 'Mercat Croce' stands within a stone-throw of the place where many strange and tragic events took

Old St Giles's.

place. Under the shadow of the venerable Kirk of St Giles this precious relic still braves the wintry blast, a reminder to the citizens and to the strangers within our gates of

stirring times that make the Scottish Capital
the envy of the world.

Memories of the Royal Mile half a century
ago arise. It may be something to boast of,
although to the 'unco guid' a rather discredit-
able admission to make, that for fifty years,
without a break, I have visited the 'Tron' on
Hogmanay. What sights of merriment and
dissipation have been witnessed during that
time! Dense crowds on every occasion, east,
west, north, and south, footing it to the dis-
cordant strains of the melodeon or bagpipes.
In one corner the familiar 'correct height and
weight' man busily plying his avocation with
marked success, while the florid face of the
portly proprietor of the 'lung tester' wears
a radiant smile as he dilates to the gaping
crowd on the good that will be derived from
a single blow! The hawker's husky cry,
'Sweet Seville oranges,' is heard above the
din. Then comes a tense stillness, and, as
the first stroke of twelve falls on the ears of
the anxious listeners, amid coloured lights,
cheering fills the air. Hands are vigorously
shaken, followed by the familiar and never-
dying wish, 'A Guid New Year, and mony
may ye see!'

Half a century ago were exciting days
for the young 'gutterbluids' of the High

Street and Canongate. 'A fire! A fire!'
is the cry as the antiquated minion of the
law emerges from the Police Office and
blows his whistle to summon the firemen
from their homes in Craig's Close and the
adjacent tall lands. A crowd of barefooted
urchins has already collected. The engine
is slowly brought into the street, and the firemen, rushing from the closes where they live,
with red helmets on their heads, and button-
ing their white trousers and blue tunics as
they come, seize the ropes! There were no
horses or motor-propelled fire-engines in
those dear old days, but, with the willing
assistance of dozens of boys, off they went
to tackle a big conflagration, say, at the
Theatre Royal!

Near Craig's Close, where the firemen had
their abode, many stirring scenes connected
with the history of Old Edinburgh have been
enacted. Almost opposite stood the Market
Cross, the hub of commercialism in the
capital at that time. On this spot there has
been many a depressing 'roup,' a strange
conglomeration of defaulters' furniture from
the hovels of the poor, seized and sold for
arrears of rent. The scene has been vividly
described in verse by James Smith, the printer-
poet, in 'The Factor and the Widow.'

The Writers' Court boys in my early days were the 'heid yins' of the High Street, and although literature of the 'Sweeney Todd' type was more to their liking than the novels of Sir Walter Scott, yet they all felt justly proud of the court where many had their homes, and of the manner in which it had been immortalised by the 'Wizard.' There in that gloomy alley was once situated Clerihugh's Tavern, and there Dandie Dinmont and the lawyer bodies from the Parliament House often met for a splore.

One of the events of my life was my meeting with Robert Louis Stevenson in Writers' Court in 1881. I had published a small book of verse in Braid Scots, and was credited with knowing something of the old houses and the old closes of the Royal Mile. Stevenson had heard of me, and, although only on a hurried visit to the city of his birth, he sought me out that summer afternoon in Writers' Court, High Street. I showed him through the quaint panelled apartment once occupied by the 'Star and Garter.' Together we made the round of once-familiar resorts.

R. L. S. was particularly interested in Advocates' Close, with its scriptural texts cut out

Clerihugh's Tavern, Writers' Court.

on the stone lintels of the doorways, and its dark turnpike stairs.

Recently an interesting correspondence appeared in the *Scotsman* regarding the place of meeting of the 'L.J.R.'—the interpretation of which is supposed to be: Liberty, Justice, and Reverence. It was a mysterious society, and Stevenson was one of the six members. According to Sir Graham Balfour (see *Life of R. L. S.*, p. 90, footnote), 'its meetings, of which only five took place, were held in a public-house situated, I believe, in Advocates' Close, which had apparently been visited by Burns.'

I can give no information concerning the abortive Essay Club, but with regard to the assertion that a public-house existed in Advocates' Close, which R. L. S., with other young bloods, frequented, I am of the opinion that there is no justification for this statement.

Even in the early days of Stevenson, Advocates' Close, with its steep declivity, was far from an inviting quarter for a 'howff' to be situated that might attract his brother Bohemians with a political or a literary turn of mind. The tall tenements on either side of the close were densely packed with poor artisans and their families, and remained so until they were demolished some years ago.

Some misconception must have arisen when the biographers of R. L. S. were compiling their books. If it had been said that the public - house was situated *near* Advocates' Close, this would have been much nearer the mark. When I visited Advocates' Close along with Stevenson, although on that occasion very communicative on things pertaining to Old Edinburgh, he never hinted that in previous years he had frequented a public-house there to discuss liberty, justice, and reverence.

John's Coffee House, in Writers' Court (not more than a stone-throw away), was visited by us. The famous 'howff' at that time was a favourite rendezvous not only for magistrates and town councillors, but also for budding advocates from the Parliament House, and a toothsome sandwich and a glass of ale could always be procured. Although this happened forty-five years ago, I have a clear recollection of what took place. Stevenson seemed to remember several of the rooms. Interrupting me, with a smile, he said, ' Not much alteration. I 've been here before, and enjoyed the splores.'

It is just possible that it was in John's

Coffee House, at the Royal Exchange, with its historic associations, and not in Advocates' Close, that the members of the Essay Club met.

St Giles, the Lawnmarket, Lady Stair's Close, Buccleuch Kirkyard (where lies the notorious Deacon Brodie), and other old houses and haunts were also visited. In George Square, after visiting No. 25, the old home of Sir Walter Scott, Stevenson asked me if I knew anything about Lord Braxfield (the Hanging Judge). I had to confess my ignorance. With a smile he turned round and, pointing up the square to the house No. 13, now occupied by the College of Agriculture, he said, 'Braxfield lived there; hot stuff in his day.' Readers of *Weir of Hermiston* will understand the significance of the remark. Probably even then Stevenson had some dim idea of using Braxfield for the purposes of fiction.

The itinerary included M'Indoo's shooting-gallery, that foul-smelling underground tunnel in Writers' Court, near the Royal Exchange. We had six shots each, and Stevenson missed the stone target twice. I was more successful, for I struck the bull's-eye and rang the bell five times, the secret being that most of my spare time was spent in M'Indoo's when a

High Street boy. The uncanny surroundings and the smell of the gunpowder must have stirred the adventurous memories of R. L. S., for he confessed to me that, although ten years my senior, he still had a hankering to write for the 'penny-bloods,' a type of literature such as *The Boys of London and New York*, to which I was contributing some pirate yarns at that time. Stories such as 'Sweeney Todd, the Demon Barber of Fleet Street,' 'Three-fingered Jack,' 'Dick Turpin,' 'David Haggart,' 'Jack Harkaway,' and 'Tom Wildrake's Schooldays' were then very popular among youthful readers. The boys' favourite hero in fiction at that time was 'Cornelius Dabber,' the timber-legged character much addicted to drinking rum. When 'Treasure Island' was published in *Young Folks*, it seemed to me that the prototype of John Silver was my old friend and hero Cornelius turned into a buccaneer.

Eventually we turned into a 'howff' not far from the Parliament House, and there, in a back room, we sat down like true Bohemians to a feast fit for the gods—hot mulled porter, saveloys, and bread.

During my lifetime it has been my good fortune to meet men and women whose names have become household words in

politics, literature, art, and music; but none
of them impressed me so much as R. L. S.
I still retain a vivid recollection of my
meeting with him in 1881. His appearance
suggested a dandified Frenchman, but the
moment he spoke his voice betrayed the true
Scots accent. His mind and actions struck
me as peculiarly boyish, and this was
thoroughly revealed during our visit to the
shooting-gallery. He revelled in the sport as
only a boy could. From the moment we met
until we parted his manner was that of one
who had known me all his life. Free from
all affectation, he seemed keenly interested in
anything I said, and his replies at times had
an element of genuine humour in them. In
short, he did not strike me as one puffed
up with his own importance, but rather the
reverse.

R. L. S. was a type of man people would
be tempted to turn round and look at if
they met him in the street. There was an
irresistible *something* which would make one
do this—possibly his eccentric style of dress,
long brown hair, and lank figure. After he
bade me good-bye, the thought occurred to
me that the genial and breezy Professor John
Stuart Blackie—for there seemed so much in
common as far as their appearance was con-

cerned—would have passed as an ideal father
to R. L. S.

In the *Weekly Scotsman*, 11th November
1911, I had a rhyming screed to a friend,
Mr Kelso Kelly, and I quote a couple of
verses which particularly refer to Stevenson :

> By Fairmilehead I took the gate
>   Where once dwelt 'Tusitala'—
> Up hill, doon howe, and, tho' 'twas late,
>   Through fields baith green and fallow.
> Stravaiging on, back to the days
>   My thochts gaed when I harkit
> To his sweet voice, and heard him praise
>   The High Street and Lawnmarket.
>
> A care-free loon was I, and deil,
>   Yet bookish, tho' fu' glaikit ;
> My hero was the lang, lean chiel
>   Wha wore the velvet jaicket !
> Sic een, sic hair, and serious look—
>   I envied Louis—raither !
> And queer, this thocht my noddle took—
>   That Blackie was his faither !

I am fully conscious that Stevenson, at
times, suffered greatly from ill-health, but I
can never get my thoughts to picture him
as a chronic invalid. That day he had the
manners of a boy—happy and full of agility.

It was in premises at the Royal Exchange,
once occupied by the famous John's Coffee

House, that the social reformers associated with the Free High Church began those pleasant Friday evenings. Dr Walter C. Smith, the poet-preacher of the Free High, realised the necessity of mission work in the High Street, and, with the assistance of the late Daniel Macfie, Thomas Lillie, and Mr Thomson of Thomson & Porteous, the penny readings from the start proved a great success. Removing later to a hall, now demolished, in Lady Stair's Close, the entertainments became more popular, some of the most eminent citizens and lecturers, including Professor Blackie, giving their services.

In the 'eighties the then unknown J. M. Barrie was dividing his ecclesiastical yearnings between the beloved ministers of Free St George's and the Free High. I have endeavoured to refresh my memory regarding Barrie at this time. As to his attendance at the 'Pleasant Evenings for Working People' I cannot vouch, but, doubtless, the young and struggling student who was qualifying for his degree, and writing an occasional article for the *Edinburgh Evening Dispatch*, did not miss the good fare at Lady Stair's Close. The foibles and frailties of humanity, as seen in the wynds and alleys of Auld Reekie, must have greatly impressed the mind and imagina-

tion of the future story-writer and dramatist
ere he journeyed south to undertake the

Lady Stair's House.

exacting work of the *Nottingham Journal* at
three guineas a week.

Now 'housed' in the old mansion in

Riddle's Close, Lawnmarket, once occupied by Bailie John Macmorran, the Penny Readings are still carried on. The year 1925 completed half a century of continuous good

Riddle's Close.

work in the Royal Mile. As a High Street boy I was present at the first meeting in the Royal Exchange, fifty years ago.

Within the memory of some living is 'Beardie' Sinclair, who was much in evidence at the 'Mercat Croce' half a century ago. He came to Edinburgh a poor boy, succeeded in business, and devoted his spare time for the good of the urchins of the Royal Mile. He also took a keen interest in Old Edinburgh and its historic traditions. He ultimately became 'Albany Herald,' and, when Royal Proclamations at the 'Croce' were more rife, his own royal appearance in gorgeous robes and his truly majestic air often gave the High Street boys the idea that the Chancellor of the Exchequer had arrived from London.

Other well-known Edinburgh 'characters' who frequented the Royal Mile at that period were 'Piper Campbell,' who sat at the old well near the head of Libberton's Wynd, and skirled the bagpipes; 'Burn-the-Bible,' a terror to all High Street bairns; 'Register Rachel,' with her quaint costume and large green umbrella; 'Curdy Glen,' the sweep; 'Blind Hughie,' the singer; 'Old Malabar,' the juggler, who gave a clever performance in Parliament Square. His great feat was to toss a solid rubber ball high into the air, and catch it in the leather cup strapped to his wrinkled forehead. 'Sour Yill' derived his nickname from his craving for sour ale, which comprised the washings of the brewers' barrels. 'Smith, the preacher,' followed in the footsteps of 'Daddy Flock-

'Old Malabar.'

hart,' although his discourses lacked the humour of his predecessor. 'Sally Kelly' was a continual source of trouble to the police, and he boasted he had a cell which was specially reserved for himself. 'Penny-a-Yard,' working assiduously at his long string of chains, was always a delight to the urchins of the Royal Mile. 'Feed the Ravens' was one of the most popular and generous of street characters. He usually stood at the Bowhead, near to the shop where Thomas Nelson, the publisher, began business. From a van laden with gingerbread he would harangue the crowd. Before selling his cakes he would break up several, and, throwing the toothsome dainty to his audience, keep on shouting, 'Feed the ravens!' He believed in the old saying, 'Taste and try before you buy.'

Other 'characters' were 'Scone Nose' the baker, 'Walking Dick,' 'Canty Muckle,' 'Pie Davie,' 'Black Mary,' and 'Apple Glory.' 'Caun'le Doups' was diminutive and bowed, and was employed as a messenger to a Nicolson Street tallow chandler. 'Mooley Heels' and 'Chew the Monkey' were noted worthies in their day. The Canongate could also boast of a number of characters. One of the most popular was 'Farthing Bob.' His little shop, under a turreted canopy, was situated near the Watergate, and his 'gundy' was known to every bairn. 'Swing Charlie,' a blind

vocalist, was another well-known 'character.'
He had a rather sweet voice, and sang, to the
accompaniment of a concertina, 'A guid New
Year to ane and a',' at the top of Waverley

'Caun'le Doups.'

Bridge on each 31st December. He derived
his nickname from his habit of swinging a
heavy stick round his body when teased by

the cry of passing urchins, 'Swing, Charlie, swing!'

In the Victorian era no other city could boast of such a curious collection of street characters as the Royal Mile.

EDINBURGH'S ANCIENT WELLS.

WHAT citizen and stranger has not gazed with curiosity at the old wells in the historic mile? From the Castlehill to the Watergate these old and battered relics of the stormy times of our forefathers have long since been a source of deep interest to more than the antiquarian.

The Watergate.

Four wells of the original five erected on the Royal Mile in 1681 still remain. The fifth one stood in front of the Weigh House or 'Butter Trone' at the head of the old West Bow, near the abode of the notorious Major Weir and his sister Grizel.

Tried for witchcraft at the Justiciary Court
in 1670, Major Weir was burned at the Gallow
Lee, Greenside, and his sister Grizel was
hanged in the Grassmarket.

The other wells in Tolbooth Wynd, Canongate; Queensberry House; foot of West Bow,
Grassmarket; Parliament Stair in the Cowgate; Guthrie Street; East Crosscauseway;

Tolbooth, Luckenbooths, and Old Well.

and Parkside Street, off St Leonard's Street,
were subsequently erected.

On proceeding from the Lawnmarket, almost
at the head of the once famous Forrester's
Wynd, stands an old well that seems to
have defied the elements. A welcome place
of rest it is for those over the three score

and ten, as well as for frowsy women, who, when the weather in Auld Reekie is on its best behaviour, watch the notables of the Parliament House hurrying to and fro. Idle clash is still carried on as in the days when the Highland porters stood there with their water-stoups, and douce burghers troked with vigour in front of their booths. If the stones of these old landmarks could only speak, what stirring tales they could tell of 'the ongauns' in the High Street!

Near to this old well may be seen in the causeway three reversed stones, marking the spot where the gibbet used to be erected in order that the last sentence of the law might be carried out. Here, on the 28th of January 1829, William Burke was taken from the lock-up and publicly executed for the atrocious West Port crimes. Many Auld Reekie citizens still remember Piper Campbell, whose favourite stance was at this well, where he skirled on the bagpipes, to the delight of Torry Gunn, the famous recruiting sergeant, and the kilties stationed at the Castle.

Within a stone-throw, Daddy Flockhart, one of the most famous of Auld Reekie's street characters, preached the gospel. At the railings of St Giles he launched his

denunciations at the loose characters of the
High Street, and declared that the only way
to put religion into the hearts of the denizens
of the Royal Mile would be by loading Mons
Meg with Bibles and firing salvation down
the Canongate !

At the head of Old Assembly Close stands
another old well. Here Bowed Joseph, that
ill-shapen specimen of humanity and leader of
the Auld Reekie mobs about 1770, assembled
his plebeian forces, and frequently worried
the hearts of the Provost and the worthy
Bailies when he marched to the Council
Chambers to seek redress for some petty
wrong. Mounted on a water-stoup at this
well, and beating his drum to draw his
followers from the alleys of the High Street,
Bowed Joseph seldom failed to accomplish
the object he had in view. A dread to those
who managed the city's affairs, his ' ongauns '
might well make the present-day law-abiding
citizens of Auld Reekie marvel at his audacious
leadership. He was a cobbler to trade, and
resided in the Cowgate ; nevertheless, by the
magnetic power of his speech and humour, he
reigned like a king, and in the popular view held
the magistrates of the Scottish Metropolis in
the hollow of his hand. Always on the rampage
for what he himself designated fair-play, he

was, in his day and generation, an idol of the people. Besieging the Town Council in their chamber in the High Street, sacking and burning in the public street the furniture of some rapacious landlord, and compelling the Grassmarket meal-dealers to sell their meal at a reasonable price to the poor, were a few of his exploits.

Those were the days of strange happenings indeed, when our rulers, to mend the matter in dispute, handed over a hogshead of good ale to Bowed Joseph to appease his rowdy followers. So popular

Bowed Joseph.

was this leader in his day that he could in an hour, by the 'touk of drum,' collect a crowd of ten thousand persons ready to follow him, or to disperse at his bidding! The end of Bowed Joseph had its tragic side. Returning from Leith races in a state of intoxication in 1780, he had a fatal fall from the top of a stage-coach.

Of the old wells in the Royal Mile, none is better known to the citizens than the one

which stands almost facing the head of
Niddry's Wynd. Close to the stair that led
to the business premises where Allan Ramsay
first became author, editor, and publisher,
this old well, iron-bound and plastered with
cement to hold its venerable stones together,
still repels the ravages of time. Luckily, it
escaped the vandal's hand when the quaint
timber-fronted land of the pastoral poet was
unfortunately demolished.

Doubtless, 'honest Allan,' like many of
our forebears who, when in their bairnhood,
were regularly
dispatched to the
poet's shop for
copies of his latest
verses, slockened
his thirst at this old
well on the warm
summer days. On
their way to St
Cecilia's Hall, to
hear the overtures
of Haydn and the
magnificent sym-
phonies of Mozart

St Cecilia's Hall.

and Beethoven, the Duchess of Gordon and
other celebrated beauties of their time must
have frequently cast their eyes on this well.

Here the merchants talked in groups side by side with Gilmerton carters bawling coal or yellow sand; fishwives from Newhaven haggled over the sale of the caller haddies in their creels; shepherds assembled in their grey plaids, and drovers stood armed to the teeth; while the old Town Guard, with their Lochaber axes, moved to and fro with laboured steps, trying to keep the more roysterous spirits in order.

Beside this well for years stood 'Cocoa-nut Tam.' Of all the Edinburgh worthies at that time he was the favourite. From his rickle of a barrow he sold fruit and cocoa-nuts. He was hump-backed and small in stature, with a thin, wrinkled face, and twinkling eyes. An old and heavy overcoat reached almost to his feet, while jauntily displayed in his billycock hat was a large sprig of heather. A picturesque object was this street-hawker, with his thin-voiced cry, 'Cocoa-nit! Cocoa-nit! A ha'penny the bit!' Thomas Simpson, for that was this well-known 'character's' name, was born in Strichen's Close, High Street, and died in the Potterrow at the age of seventy-one years.

Strange as it may seem, Robert Louis Stevenson, although he must have frequently passed this old well in his university days, had no recollection of 'Cocoa-nut Tam.' In a letter to me from Samoa in 1894, he says, 'Cocoa-nut Tam, though it argue me unknown myself, I do not seem to be able to place, unless he were an honest merchant at the head of the Lawn Market!'

Here Jamie M'Levy, the famous detective, might also have been seen on the lookout for his 'bairns' as they emerged from their haunts in Blackfriars Wynd, at that time one of the most dangerous and disreputable alleys of the city. Perched on the top of this old well when the occasion arose, gutterbluids from the High Street used to watch with joy the procession of the Lord High Commissioner from the Palace to the Assembly Hall. On other occasions their young hearts swelled with martial ardour as the 'sodgers' marched down the historic street.

At John Knox's House, another old well arrests the eye. Visitors to the abode of the great Scottish reformer, particularly the globe-trotter thirsting for information, have often stood with guide-book in hand, gazing at this relic. Meagre indeed are the particulars of its history. Nevertheless, it remains as a monument recording the quaint and obsolete manner in which the douce citizens of the Scottish capital obtained their water. How primitive compared with the present-day ' well in-the-hoose,' whose unlimited supply from the reservoir of the Talla is often, I fear, not fully appreciated.

It is recorded that it was no uncommon thing to see the youngest sister of the beautiful Duchess of Gordon engaged in carrying water from the fountain-well for tea. At that period the Duchess was the leader of fashionable society in Edinburgh, and lived with her mother and sisters in Hyndford's Close (where Sir Walter Scott was made a Freemason later). If the stones of this old well could speak, what a description they could give of

Hyndford's Close.

the harrowing scenes on that Sunday morning on the 10th of November 1861, when the High Street land fell, and buried in its ruins thirty-five poor dwellers, among them being the brave boy, Joseph M'Ivor, who cried to those who were digging out the dead and wounded : 'Heave awa', chaps, I 'm no deid yet !'

Not farther back than the 'sixties and 'seventies this old well was the favourite rendezvous of the Canongate hawkers, who turned this part of the Royal Mile into a veritable inferno with their flaring paraffin lamps and raucous voices, as they stood by their well-laden barrows and baskets proclaiming the price of ' chippit apples, Irish dulse, bluidy puddin's, and cheena bowls !' Saturday night at the Netherbow Well was a never-to-be-forgotten sight, and many are still alive who can vividly remember the almost indescribable scenes enacted there.

Almost at the foot of the Canongate, with its stirring memories of the past, the well outside the wall of Queensberry House is still an object of interest, although erected at a later date. This well is overlooked by the famous mansion which in 1801, by the orders of the *blasé* ' Old Q,' was stripped of its beautiful decorations and sold to the Government to be used as a barrack. The fifty-eight rooms, and noble gallery seventy feet long, where intrigue and tragedy were fostered by dukes and duchesses, now serve a useful purpose as a house of refuge for the destitute and as an inebriates' home. The poor denizens of the adjacent tall lands must frequently have watched from their windows their gossiping neighbours at the well below, redding up the idle clash of the previous day, and many an amazon with tousled hair had cause to remember her fisticuff encounter with her randy opponent at the Watergate Well. Such incidents, luckily, are now a thing of the past, and the Royal Mile, except on a Saturday night, has lost much of its characteristic 'steer,' and is usually as quiet as a village street.

These wells still remind us of the crude conditions that existed in the domestic life of the people in the days of auld langsyne, when the carrying of the water-stoups must have been a lucrative trade for the Highland porters. May the old wells long remain in Auld Reekie as interesting relics of the past—a reminder to generations yet to come of the primitive times in which their forefathers lived.

THE OLD 'FREE=AND=EASIES.'

MUCH might be written about the social side of Edinburgh half a century ago. Compared with the present time, one can truthfully exclaim: 'Changed days, indeed!' In the Victorian era the citizens of Auld Reekie took their enjoyments simply; places of amusement were comparatively few. Good fare at that time in the shape of legitimate drama was being provided at the Theatre Royal, the old Princess, and at the South-minster.

Music-halls at that time were in their infancy, the old Gaiety in Chambers Street being the one and only place of entertainment. Some kind of light entertainment seemed to be desired by the men-folk, and the power of good and catchy songs was revealed in the many 'free-and-easies' which sprang up, mushroom-like, throughout the city. Almost every public-house that could boast of a back room large enough had a piano, and, particularly on a Saturday night, smoking concerts, or, as they were more familiarly termed, 'free-and-easies,' were held.

Bryce's, at 63 Princes Street, now occupied by Durie Brown's, was one of the most popular and best conducted in Edinburgh. Here, in a long subterranean room, where the light of day was unable to penetrate, a 'sing-song' was nightly held, and the efforts of the obliging frequenters were usually far from the mediocre order. Norman Thomson, the portly chairman of Bryce's, was a well-known basso in his day. He sat at a little round table at the far end of the room, and a rap from his hammer, or 'Order, order, gentle-men!' from his stentorian voice, was always sufficient to bring about the silence desired when a singer was about to 'oblige.'

The frequenters of this convivial howff were chiefly of the commercial class—shopkeepers and clerks, with a sprinkling of beardless middies, and spurred horse-soldiers from Jock's Lodge in their scarlet tunics and gold braid-ings. The comic songs sung were usually those that had just become popular in the London music-halls, while sentimental and patriotic ditties never failed to receive the well-deserved encores. Dibdin's 'Tom Bowling,' 'Rocked in the Cradle of the Deep,' 'The Diver,' and a song in praise of Samuel Plimsoll, the sailors' friend, were favourites with Jack. The power of the Navy was as much appreci-ated in those days as at the present time, as 'The Union Jack of old England,' the chorus of which went with a fine swing, can testify :

> The flag that cheers our sailors on their way,
> The flag that fills our foes with dismay,
> The flag that always carries the sway,
> It's the Union Jack of Old England !

This patriotic song was very popular, and was sung by Joe Simpson, a printer, who had a fine, cultured voice, and a Byronic face. The daring deeds of 'Tommy,' too, received their meed of praise, and 'Let me Like a Soldier Fall,' 'The Battle of Stirling Bridge,' or verses in honour of General Gordon, the hero of Khartoum, aroused the military enthusiasm of the 'old campaigners,' who, if they were of a temperate turn of mind, could have their two or three hours' entertainment for the sum of fourpence, the charge that was made for a large glass of beer.

It was at Bryce's that R. S. Pillans, the well-known Scottish comedian, for many years a great pantomime favourite at the Theatre Royal with his topical songs, made his début. Sixty years ago, as an outlet for his mimicry, this young 'devil' from an adjoining printing-house doubtless found the Princes Street 'free-and-easy' more congenial to his taste than the setting of type or the clanking noise of cylinder printing-machines.

Many frequenters of Bryce's who have settled down in lands 'ayont the sea' will have happy recollections of evenings spent in the Princes Street 'free-and-easy,' and of the artistes whose names were then a household word in Auld Reekie. Scottish comedians were always well to the front—Willie Cummings, a pioneer of pawky Scots patter, long before Sir Harry Lauder was ever heard of; also R. P. Jennings and J. H. Gilchrist; Tom Walker and James Bradley, baritones. The comic element was well sustained by W. L. Christison, Ted Watson, W. Joss, and James Glass; J. Reid, tenor; and Charles Dunnigan could be relied upon to give a faithful rendering of Charles Godfrey's 'Here upon Guard am I!' Others included Peter Cockburn, who sang 'The Diver'; Peter Stachini was frequently called upon to give his imitation of birds; and Bill Joss, the latest songs of Arthur Roberts. Fred Lindsay, a newspaper-compositor, gave a very effective rendering of the then popular chorus:

It is a wondrous story, proclaim it far and wide,
And let your children's children re-echo it with pride,
How Cardigan, the fearless, his name immortal made,
As he swept the Russian valley with his famous Light
    Brigade.

Other great favourites when Norman Thomson controlled the destinies of Bryce's 'free-and-easy' were:

> Tommy, make room for your uncle, there's a little dear;
> Never mind the school, boy, go for a pint of beer—
> You know your ma has got a bun, and that she'll give to you;
> So, don't annoy, be a good boy, make room for your uncle, do.

And the racing song, that always appealed to the devotees of the turf:

> We have jockeys young and old, we have jockeys smart and bold,
> Both tall and crooked jockeys we have got,
> And all of them, of course, know how to ride a horse,
> But Fred Archer, he's the king of all the lot.

All of the 'free-and-easies' were presided over by chairmen, but the name of one in particular is still remembered with a fervour bordering upon enthusiasm—the one and only Norman Thomson, of Bryce's 'free-and-easy.'

A shoemaker to trade, young Thomson soon discovered that he had an exceptionally fine bass voice, and his rendering of such old favourites as 'The Macgregor's Gathering,' 'The Wolf,' 'Annie on the Banks o' Dee,' and 'O' a' the Airts' soon brought him into prominence in musical circles. The position of chairman of Bryce's in Princes Street having become vacant, he applied for the post, and was successful. Incredible as it may seem, this position was held for almost thirty years! During his long tenure of office no howff in Auld Reekie was better known than Bryce's.

I am the possessor of many curiosities associated with Old Edinburgh, including the little wooden hammer that Norman Thomson used for thirty years in Bryce's 'free-and-easy.' This may not be a relic worth preserving in the Corporation Museum, but if the hammer could only speak, what a tale it could tell of conviviality in the days of our youth! As a reminder of the 'guid auld days,' thousands would doubtless like to have a 'keek' at this wee hammer that would recall happy memories of auld langsyne.

Thousands who fancied themselves capable of entertaining the frequenters of Bryce's must have responded to the call of Norman Thomson during his long period as chairman. Even to-day, some of those who are looked upon as staid City Fathers have confessed to me that the happiest hours in the days of their youth were spent in the Princes Street 'free-and-easy.'

John Norman, otherwise known as Norman Thomson, was born at Edinburgh in 1837. He died in 1899, in his sixty-second year, and was buried in Warriston Cemetery. Bryce's 'free-and-easy' was closed in 1896, three years before he died. It can truthfully be said that, in his own particular sphere, no one was better known in Auld Reekie half a century ago than Norman Thomson.

A feature of Bryce's in Norman Thomson's time was the orchestra. Although few in number, the ability of the musicians was never doubted by the singers who were called upon to 'oblige.' John Inglis officiated at the piano, with Willie Sangster as occasional deputy; Joe Hart was violinist. The men of the orchestra were born masters in their profession as accompanists, and never required the music-sheet.

The south side of Edinburgh could boast of Mother Anderson's, at the corner of Cross-causeway, and Forsyth's in Hill Place, where John M'Naughton was chairman, and Fred Wallace, a Tyrolean vocalist, always 'scored'; while the denizens of the High School Yards and Cowgate found vocal entertainment in a howff in Infirmary Street.

To come nearer the Tron, White's, at the head of the old North Bridge, was well known

in its day—the actual part of the land where
Allan Ramsay, the poet, successfully carried
on his wig-making and song-writing. Many,
no doubt, visited this noted 'free-and-easy'
out of mere curiosity. Entering from the

Head of old North Bridge.

pavement with the assistance of a thick brass
hand-rail, you descended a dozen steps, and
found yourself in a long cellar similar to
Bryce's in Princes Street. The entertainment was conducted on much the same lines,
with the exception of the chairman's authority,

which the rowdy 'Canongoshans' frequently treated with contempt.

Other much-frequented 'free-and-easies' were in Cockburn Street and Milne Square. Tam Niven's, in the Fleshmarket, strictly speaking, was more of a howff, where 'sairly trauchled wives,' enjoying a Saturday night's outing with their guidmen, adjourned to 'hae a gless o' ale' and a toothsome sandwich, for which the shop was famous.

Songs of a patriotic, descriptive motto and topical nature had great vogue in the 'guid auld days.' One introduced by R. S. Pillans, in the Theatre Royal, about 1868, was as follows:

> I ance was young and fresh and fair,
>   But noo I 'm auld and yellow ;
> Auld Scotland is my native place—
>   I was born in Portobello !
> I crossed the seas to marry my Joe,
>   Wha had settled oot in Indy ;
> But he was marrit when I got there,
>   Sae we had a bit o' a shindy !'

Germany and France were not on the friendliest terms at that time, as the following will show:

> Germany is said to be funky with fright ;
>   Keep it dark !
> She fancies that France is preparing to fight ;
>   Keep it dark !

Then there was a love ditty, 'If ever I Cease to Love'; and 'the Store' did not escape criticism in 'Co-operation':

> We've Co-operative cloth, Co-operative silk,
> Co-operative cows to give Co-operative milk;
> Co-operative parasols, and also wooden legs,
> Co-operative hens to lay Co-operative eggs;
> Co-operative raisins, and Co-operative figs,
> Co-operative sausages, Co-operative pigs!

A 'number' that had been sung into popularity by a London comique was another great favourite:

> Gold, gold, gold, I love to hear it jingle,
> Gold, gold, gold, its power is untold;
> We men strive hard to store it, and women they
>   adore it,
> The best friend that a man can have is gold, gold,
>   gold.

'That's what Puzzles the Quaker,' 'Schneider, How you Vas?' 'The Yorkshire Lass,' 'Grandfather's Clock,' 'My Auld Grannie's Leather Pouch,' 'Nancy Lee,' 'Bonnie Fairy Mary,' and many others were regularly sung at the 'free-and-easies.' The songs of Tom Bowling, a motto vocalist, who appeared at the old Gaiety in Chambers Street with 'Where was Moses when the Light Went Out?' and 'A

Penny and the Bob,' were always 'picked up'
by the local singers.

> When you 've got a penny, boys,
>   Never be too willing ;
> Although it is a paltry coin,
>   It helps to make a shilling.
> When you 've got a shilling, boys,
>   Spin it round and round ;
> Never spend it foolish,
>   That 's the way to save a pound.

There was also much sound advice in the
following :

> Let the world jog on as it may,
> Always strive to be happy and gay ;
> Always do right, and never do wrong
> As you paddle your boat along.

Many old and respected citizens of Auld
Reekie must still remember the 'pleasures'
of an evening spent in a vitiated atmosphere of smoke, where, to the accompaniment of a wheezy piano and a fiddle, they
listened to songs beloved of the 'free-
and-easies.' Like the clubs and taverns of
our forefathers, those institutions seem to
have supplied a felt want, but they are now
only a memory of the past.

A FAMOUS PRINTING-HOUSE.

THE old wooden printing-press that for many years stood at the entrance hall of Paul's works, Causewayside, Edinburgh, and attracted sympathetic attention from many visitors, recalls several incidents that came under my personal notice. Being a Ballantonian, and having a hankering after 'the literary life,' during my apprenticeship I had the privilege of a closer friendship with one of my employers, the late Mr Edward Hanson, than is usually supposed to exist between master and man. Mr Hanson's visits from London were neither frequent nor prolonged, but on almost every occasion he found time not only to encourage me in my literary ventures, but to introduce me to literary celebrities who were being shown through the works.

Mr Andrew Lang—' dear Andrew with the brindled hair '—I vividly recall at this moment. At the time, if I rightly remember, the firm was printing a superb library edition of the works of Sir Walter Scott for J. C. Nimmo, of London, and it was being edited by Mr Lang. Strange to say, during the conversation I had with him, and in the presence of

Mr Edward Hanson, the history of the old wooden press cropped up. Judged not only by his business capacity, but his love for all that pertained to the Ballantyne Press, no one, I venture to say, was more able to pronounce on the genuineness or otherwise of the press than Mr Hanson. I particularly noted his answers to Mr Lang, being, as I then was, deeply interested in the subject, for, when a lad, I not only helped to work the press in question at the International Exhibition held at Edinburgh in 1886, but penned a rhyming tribute, which as a throw-away leaflet was printed on the old press. Regarding the authenticity of the press, I distinctly remember Mr Hanson saying to Mr Lang that 'it was *generally supposed* that the press had actually printed some of the sheets of the original editions of the Waverley Novels.' I have italicised the words 'generally supposed' because Mr Andrew Lang seemed a bit surprised. I also felt keenly disappointed at Mr Hanson's remark, having up till then had no reason to doubt the genuineness of the relic.

I was determined, however, to inquire further into the matter. Being an intimate literary friend of the late Mr W. T. Dobson, author of *Royal Characters of Scott*, who for

a great number of years acted as reader at
Paul's Work, I mentioned the Lang incident,
certain that no one in the office, with the
exception of Mr Edward Hanson, was more
to be relied on regarding the facts. Mr
Dobson's answer also astonished me. With
a smile, he said: 'Sometimes it's no' wise to
inquire too closely into the history of things—
especially if one's of a romantic turn of mind!'
'But,' I replied, 'at the time of the Edinburgh
Exhibition my verses on the advertising leaflet
you prepared must have led people to believe
that the old wooden press was used by
Ballantyne in the printing of Scott's novels.'
I was then laughingly reminded that poets
were allowed a certain licence, and, taking the
leaflet in question from his desk (I still have
the copy in my possession), he drew my
attention to the fact that his own wording
of the relics to be seen 'at ye prenting shop
frae Paul's Work' ran thus:

*'Among the many curious and interesting
objects to be here seen, the following may be
mentioned:*

'Old Wooden Printing Press (*as used* by
Ballantyne in printing Scott's Novels).

'Sir Walter Scott's Desk and Chair.

'Ink Balls, or Dabbers.

'Old Composing-Sticks and Mallet.

'Rules and Directions for Printing Offices (1721).

'Chapel Snuff Mull, &c. &c.'

Will lovers of the 'Wizard' please note that Mr Dobson distinctly says 'Sir Walter Scott's desk and chair,' which ought to remove all doubt as to the genuineness of these precious relics.

Shattered convictions are 'ill to thole,' and, still hoping that I might yet be able to score on the point, I then consulted the late Mr Samuel Kinnear, another press-reader at Paul's Work, who was a bit of an antiquarian, and well known in his day as the author of *The King's Printing House in Blair Street*. His opinion was characteristic of the kindly old man. 'If I had been in the Canongate when Sir Walter's novels were being printed, I wad hae been able to tell ye; but, as far as the press doon the stair is concerned, I hae my doots!'

Somehow after that the old wooden press never had the same attraction for me, although I admired it as a relic of a bygone time when the Auld Reekie craftsmen, with their un-bounded enthusiasm for good workmanship, were making a name for themselves that to the present day has been worthily sustained,

Antique it undoubtedly is, and, if for no other reason than as a reminder of old habits and old traditions, a fitting place for the press would be a National Museum, to avert the possibility of its being some day thrown upon the scrap-heap of worn-out things. Sir Walter Scott's desk and chair, and the old wooden printing press, were removed to London when the Ballantyne Press, Edinburgh, closed down in 1915.

Scott's familiar lines, with an apt variation:

> Breathes there a man with soul so dead
> Who never to himself hath said :
> 'In Ballantyne's the dons are bred'?

used to be much quoted at Paul's Work in my youthful days.

Dons undoubtedly were bred in the famous printing-house in Causewayside in those happy although laborious times for compositors and pressmen. Trades Unionism and Factory Act restrictions were not much in evidence then. As far as the printers and the working of overtime were concerned, it was simply 'go as you please'! So chronic had this become that it is related of an old craftsman, who never got home during the week before his bairns were all in bed and asleep, that when Sunday came round they used to say, 'Mither, what strange man is that in oor hoose?'

As to the extent to which 'dab' (*i.e.* overtime) might be carried on in those days, it may be mentioned that when Lord Beaconsfield died in 1881 an order came from London for the immediate printing of a complete set of the statesman's novels. By working at high pressure on a few presses, the whole of the seventeen volumes were turned out in six days, several of the printers, the writer included, having no less than fifty hours' overtime to their credit!

My earliest recollections go back more than fifty years to John Oswald, a prince of readers in deciphering manuscripts that often proved the despair of the much-worried comps. It was my duty, as reading-boy, to sit in the small 'box,' with scarcely room to move, beside that highly-trained worthy, whose swear-words (for John never hesitated to call a spade a spade when at his wits' end as to the identity of some Hebrew or Greek hieroglyphics, or the almost unreadable writing of Andrew Lang) used to strike terror into the heart of every apprentice.

It was a welcome relief to the reading-boy when informed by Mr Grut, the caseroom overseer, or 'Tam' Scott, who had charge of

the apprentices, that his services were required
by Mr Bishop, or 'G. D. B.', as he was
familiarly named by all at Paul's Work.
Comparisons are odious, but it must be confessed that to read to 'G. D. B.' was a pleasure
instead of a task. His cheery presence and
kindly manner made him first favourite with
the printers' 'devils,' and those who are still
left will ever remember his snatches of old
Scots songs between-times, for 'Geordie' was
no mean exponent of the matchless lyrics
of our country, and was well known as a
lecturer on such in his day. Mr George
D. Bishop and the writer at that time were
bosom cronies of 'Jamie' Smith, the printer-
poet and story-writer, and a night with
those worthy old craftsmen could never be
forgotten.

Boys will be boys, and many of the high
jinks played on 'Davie' Gardner, the crabbit
proof pressman of the caseroom, usually
resulted in a 'court-martial' before Mr James
Mossman, the manager. Stern and un-
bending, he nevertheless had many qualities
that endeared him to all. During his long
tenure of office as manager of Paul's Work
his responsibilities were great, but the
apprentices and journeymen knew that the
craft was safe, and would weather any storm

under the guidance of such a straightforward
and practical skipper.

Proud of the position he occupied, he often
spoke to the writer about the great changes
that had taken place since James Ballantyne
came to Edinburgh from Kelso with 'his
two presses and a proof one,' and the rapid
development of the firm since its removal
from the old Physic Gardens in the Canongate to Causewayside. Doubtless, also, the
founder and the great Sir Walter would have
felt a justifiable pride in knowing that the
Ballantyne Press at that period was still at
the front in the swift race that was being run
in the world's business, and, like Dominie
Sampson, would have been ready to exclaim
'Prodigious!'

Old wooden presses had already given
place to the more modern iron Columbian,
and many of these simple but reliable presses
were under the control of 'Geordie' Thom,
an expert in his time at the making-up of
overlays for the woodcuts which were then
very much in vogue. An artist in his work,
he was entrusted with the printing of the
limited number of impressions that were
required from Thomas Bewick's masterpiece
in wood engraving, 'The Chillingham Bull'
(1789), before it was destroyed. Assisting

this worthy old craftsman at the press, I well remember examining the precious cracked woodcut, and how, Sherlock Holmes like, he watched that no 'extra' copy of this valuable print might be 'pulled,' and surreptitiously carried away from the works.

Later on, and during the absence of 'Geordie' owing to illness, it was my good fortune to throw-off from the hand press that remarkable volume, *The City of Dreadful Night, and other Poems*, by James Thomson, 'B.V.,' published by Reeves & Turner, London, 1880. 'Dreadful' nights to me they were in more ways than one, for—being then a novice in the 'black airt'—in my sleepless hours after the sheets had been dispatched to the publishers, I always had a dread of some complaint about the 'register' or the 'colour.'

Migrating to the machine-room proper, under the charge of Adam Govan, with its old creaking platens and Brown cylinders, which have since been superseded by fast revolution presses of French and German make, I had the honour of being entrusted with the printing of the entire five volumes of Ruskin's *Modern Painters* (large paper copy), published by George Allan, Orpington, 1892. That was, indeed, to me a labour

of love all through, and I needed no reminder
from the overseer to 'tak' my time, and mak'
a guid job o 't.' 'It is a typographical credit
to the Ballantyne Press,' were the words of
the late Mr Edward Hanson to me afterwards, 'and Mr John Ruskin asked me to
convey his thanks to you.' This was high
praise from the great writer.

The convivial meetings of the Ballantyne
chapel in those days were events to be remembered.   Kindred spirits forgathered at weel-
kent howffs in the Fleshmarket Close, Mrs
Gilchrist's in Milne Square, Mother Anderson's
at the Crosscauseway, the Melville Hotel,
Nicolson Street, or the 'Peacock' at Newhaven, and many a splore was indulged in
till 'Some wee short hour ayont the twal.'
'Pay-offs' by the new journeymen and Burns
suppers were red-letter nights.   Between the
haggis, the toasts, and the skirl of the bagpipes, appreciation of James Ballantyne, Sir
Walter Scott, and the Ballantyne Press was
never forgotten.

Most of these honoured worthies are gone
—craftsmen who played no unworthy part
in helping to make the printing industry of
Edinburgh known the world o'er.

AULD EDINBURGH 'CRIES.'

OLD Edinburgh memories would not be complete without some reference to the quaint street cries that used to greet the ear in the days of our grandfathers.

With the exception of the raucous voice of the coalman, who is still in our midst, present-day citizens of Auld Reekie desiring quietness have much to be thankful for. For centuries Auld Reekie has been famous for its street 'cries.' The enormous strides made in public health and sanitation make one shudder at the thought of the conditions under which our forefathers lived in the days of 'Gardy-loo!' In the wynds and closes of the Royal Mile in the sixteenth and seventeenth centuries this well-known 'warning' struck terror to the heart of every passer-by. In those days the aristocratic dwellers in the High Street practised the simple plan of shooting all household refuse over the windows instead of carrying it down the narrow turnpike stairs.

'Gardyloo' was a familiar nightly cry, and the roysterers of that drunken period— for almost every close in the High Street had its tavern or howff—ran great risks not only by reason of unsteady limbs, but from what

might fall upon their heads. Those unable
to pronounce the corrupted French phrase
('Beware of the water') gave warning in
broad Scots — 'Get out o' the gait!' In
those days the Royal Mile was a veritable
midden-heap. Fruit, vegetables, fish, flesh,
and fowl were exposed for sale, and carriers'
horses added to the confusion of the crowded
thoroughfare. Even herds of swine roamed
at large, and it is narrated that the beautiful
Duchess of Gordon, as a girl, careered
about the Netherbow on the back of a
pig!

Many still alive will remember, and perhaps
regret, the passing of a custom which at one
time greatly prevailed, and which proved such
a convenience to the thrifty housewives of
Auld Reekie. In the poorer localities, in
'the guid auld days,' the flesher's cart from
the 'killing hoose' was eagerly awaited, and
a roaring trade was done. How the women
folk to-day must envy their grannies who, for
sixpence, could procure a large sheep's head
and trotters—sufficient, if made into broth, to
feed a family for three days in the week. I
can remember the well-known cry, 'Sheep's
heids, buy them up!' And buy them up
the denizens of the Lawnmarket, High Street,
and Canongate undoubtedly did. The butter-
milk cart was familiar to everyone, and 'Fine

soor-dook, a penny the pint!' found a ready

Carter in the Canongate.

sale. A large dish of 'garvies' could be purchased for a penny. The hawkers did not trouble to weigh the edible sprats in those days. From a heavily-laden cart they were shovelled into the buyer's basin!

During summer, on the green slopes of the Queen's Park near St Anthony's Well, a never-to-be-forgotten sight was the women, with well-polished pails, crying, 'Curds and whey!' 'Rosy-cheekit aipples, the rale Carse o' Gowries,' and 'Ripe berries, the big pint a ha'penny,' were also in great demand by the artisan crowds that frequented this charming spot. 'Neeps like succar, braw, big neeps,' were a bawbee the piece, and 'Bonnie caller radishes,' four bunches a penny. 'Berries, green and yellow,' and 'Sugar plooms, baith sweet and fine,' ever found a ready customer at a halfpenny the pint. Vendors of 'heather ranges' were daily to be met, and the popularity of the 'Heather Jocks' has been celebrated in a humorously descriptive song:

> Heather Jock 's noo awa',
> Heather Jock 's noo awa';
> The muircock noo may crousely craw,
> Since Heather Jock 's noo awa'.
> Heather Jock was stark and grim,
> Focht wi' a' would fecht wi' him;
> Swank and supple, sharp and thin,
> Fine for gaun against the win'!

Tawnie face and tousie hair,
In his cleedin' unco bare ;
Cursed and swore whene'er he spoke—
Nane could equal Heather Jock.

The 'Heather Jocks' were often accompanied by far from prepossessing specimens of humanity, crying 'Candy rock, candy rock!' that never failed to delight the bairns. Home products in a way held their own with the limited 'delicacies' then imported. 'Peas and beans, warm and hot!' and 'Caller partans, big and sma'!' satisfied the most epicurean taste; while 'Haddies, caller haddies, fresh and lowpin' in the creel!' could always be bought at an insignificant price.

Of all the traders' cries that re-echoed through the streets of Auld Reekie none was more popular than that of picturesque Fisher Jenny, immortalised by the Baroness Nairne in the beautiful song of 'Caller Herrin'.' We are told that the lyric was based 'upon the cry of the Newhaven fishwives, who, clad in short heavy dresses of dark blue flannel, carried their fish in creels supported on their backs and braced to their foreheads with bands of leather. These sturdy women perambulated the streets of Auld Reekie, selling their fish from door to door, in all quarters of the city. They proclaimed their mission

with voices that might put to shame an
organ on the highest of wind pressures, and
submitted to any amount of chaffing and
cheapening of their wares.'

> Buy my caller herrin',
> They 're bonnie fish and halesome farin';
> Buy my caller herrin',
>> New drawn frae the Forth.

Nathaniel Gow, son of the famous Neil,
was the composer of the air. In 1782 he
became one of His Majesty's Trumpeters for
Scotland, and in 1791 succeeded his brother
as leader of the fashionable concerts at
Edinburgh. He subsequently engaged in
the music-publishing business, and died at
Edinburgh in 1831.

Another 'cry' that has been handed down
in imperishable verse is 'Caller Ou!'

> When winter winds howl,
>> And the sea 's rolling high,
> Our laddies sae brave
>> All dangers defy.
> The last haul on board,
>> As they steer to the shore,
> The live cargo landed
>> Is soon at the door.
>>> Caller ou! Caller ou!
>>> Caller ou frae the Forth!
>>> Caller ou! Caller ou!

In summer time, when the gray steeple of St Giles' brightened in the sunshine, bare-footed lassies, with heavily-laden baskets, were daily to be seen, and ' Buy my bonnie water-cresses, a' the road frae Loudon Burn!' or their melodious cry, ' Come awa, come awa!' greeted the ear at every turn. From the wrathful look on the faces of ' Penny-a-yard,' or the auld wife selling ' Laces, laces, strong leather laces, a bawbee the pair!' at the Tron, it was evident those well-known High Street worthies did not believe in the maxim that competition is the life of trade. Never-theless, they managed to eke out a decent living.

A particularly busy quarter was the head of Niddry's Wynd, where the carriers' carts arrived in the morning with their tempting dairy produce in the shape of new-laid eggs, and rolls of fresh butter daintily wrapped in a cabbage-blade for the carrying away. Early risers were there in force to haggle with the seller over the price of a live hen or duck, which a few hours later might be seen strut-ting in front of the buyer's dwelling-place in Cowgate or Grassmarket! There were fewer poultry restrictions in those ' dear auld days' to worry the thrifty housewives domiciled in Auld Reekie, and it was no uncommon sight to see a pig or a butting nanny-goat wandering about the streets.

From morning till night in St Mary's Wynd, which, until the year 1869, was a narrow stifling alley full of brokers' shops, and where, in 1773, Dr Samuel Johnson, on his memorable tour to the Hebrides, lodged at Boyd's Inn, hawkers with their carts plied a busy trade in 'Cauf for beds' and 'Yellow sand.' Under the improvement Act of 1867 the whole of the wretched slums on its eastern side were swept away, and the wynd became a broad and spacious thoroughfare.

Still to be seen are the lassies with their creels, selling the delectable boiled 'whulks and buckies' at a penny the plate. They commonly take their stand at the door of some public-house on a Saturday afternoon in a busy thoroughfare, such as the High Street or Leith Street, where they find Tommy and Jack ever-ready customers. At the Fair, when the 'Glesca buddies' invade Portobello—our Brighton of the North—here also the indefatigable mussel-wife holds her own on the sands with the vendor of the 'slider' and other mysterious 'dainties.'

Gone, never again to be recalled, are the 'Auld Edinburgh Cries,' yet to many who

still love the old order of things they will
remain a cherished memory.

NOTED CLUBS AND TAVERNS.

OF perennial interest to the Scot at home
and abroad is everything that pertains
to Auld Reekie and its people in what have
been described as 'the good old days.' Many
however, who have made a critical study of
some of the noted clubs and taverns, and of
the bacchanalian orgies that nightly took place
within their walls, may well 'hae their doots!'

It is recorded that tavern-dissipation more
than a century ago prevailed in Edinburgh to
an incredible extent, and
engrossed the leisure hours
of all professional men.
No rank or class formed
an exception to this rule.
'Nothing was so common
in the morning as to meet
a nobleman or two reeling
from a close in the High
Street, where they had
spent the whole night in

Jovial Lords of Session.

drinking. Nor was it unusual to find the half
of His Majesty's most honourable Lords of

Council and Session mounting the bench in the forenoon in a drunken state!'

Than Robert Fergusson, the luckless poet, no one has given a more vivid description of the deep carousals that took place. In his address to 'Auld Reekie' he graphically says:

> Auld Reekie! wale o' ilka toon
> That Scotland kens beneath the moon;
> Where couthy chiels at e'enin' meet
> Their bizzin' craigs and mou's to weet,
> And blythely gar auld care gae by,
> Wi' blinkin' and wi' blearin' eye.

The howffs where our convivial forefathers forgathered have—happily—been swept away, but the curiosities of Old Edinburgh and the peculiarities of its people at that time will ever remain green in the hearts of per-fervid Scots.

In the thoroughfare from the Castle to the Watergate, including some of the adjacent wynds, most of the clubs and taverns were situated. Farther afield, in the Potterrow, however, there was located a quaint public-house and huckster's shop kept by Lucky Fykie, who is supposed to have been the prototype of Mrs Flockhart, immortalised by Sir Walter Scott in *Waverley*. Her stock-in-trade consisted of ropes, tea, sugar, whip-

handles, porter, ale, butter, sand, caum-stane,
herrings, nails, cotton-wicks, papers, pens, ink,
wafers, thread, needles, tapes, potatoes, gundy,
onions, spunks, and coloured eggs—an assort-
ment of articles which any present-day small
grocer might be proud to own. But picture
the father of Sir Walter Scott, Lord Braxfield (the hanging judge of Robert Louis
Stevenson's *Weir of Hermiston*), Mr Dundas,
afterwards Lord Melville, and most of the
lawyers who lived in George Square and the
other southern suburbs, dropping into this
howff daily in passing home from the Court,
to regale themselves with a dram from the
auld wife's bottle! Sir Walter's father was
a regular customer of Lucky Fykie's for
many years. It was principally in the historic
mile that bacchanalian revelry held sway, and
the Lawnmarket Club was composed of the
woollen-traders of that street, who met at
seven o'clock in the morning, and marched
to the post-office to get the latest London
news. An adjournment to a favourite howff
followed.

The Spendthrift Club, where members were
committed to the spending of no less a sum
than fourpence-halfpenny each night, was also
located in Wardrop's Court, Lawnmarket.
There, over a game of halfpenny whist,

respectable merchants enjoyed their farles of
cakes, tripe and buffed haddock, 'syned doon'
with a tankard of reeming ale, all of which
cost no more than fivepence, including a halfpenny to the serving lass! Wives of to-day
are better circumstanced than then, for no
business man thought of going home to his
'ain fire-end' till after he had spent two or
three hours at his club.

Johnnie Dowie's tavern in Libberton's Wynd
was one of the howffs where Burns met
kindred spirits when he visited Auld Reekie.
Other literary lights, like Christopher North
and Thomas Campbell, sampled the barley-
bree in Johnnie's tavern. What
splores must have taken place in
that dark and narrow alley!

One sidelight will be sufficient.
'A gentleman one night stepped
into Johnnie Dowie's, and, looking into a room, saw a heap of
snoring drunks upon the floor,
while the gleam of an expiring
candle illumined the wreck and
debris of a perfect pitched battle
of Bacchus. "Wha may thae
be, Mr Dowie?" inquired the
visitor. "Oh," answered Johnnie, in his usual
quiet imperturbable way, "just twa-three o'

Johnnie Dowie.

Sir William's drucken clerks!"—meaning the gentlemen employed in the banking-house of Sir William Forbes, who, of all earthly mortals, one would have expected to be decent fellows.'

In Writers' Court, where the west wing of the new municipal buildings now stands, was the 'Star and Garter,' which was kept by Clerihugh. The tavern has been immortalised by Sir Walter Scott in *Guy Mannering* as the howff where Pleydell met the lawyer bodies from the Parliament House. In those days it was also the chief resort of the Edinburgh Magistrates, whose 'high jinks,' if now carried on, would bring the blush of shame to the cheeks of our City Fathers.

The curious-minded of to-day, turning into Craig's Close, 'almaist fornenst the Mercat Cross,' should pause at the old tenement which faces the High Street, for there on the first flat of that high land, No. 257, may still be seen the unpretentious office, with the lettering yet visible on the lintel, where the *Scotsman* was published from 1826 to 1864. Prior to this date the office was at 347 High Street, from which the *Scotsman* was originally issued. A year later the office was transferred to 166 High Street.

Here also stood the booth of Andro

Hart, the famous old Scottish printer, whose
well-known Bible proves what masters of
their art were the craftsmen of long ago.   It
was in Craig's Close, dangerous in its declivity
—the tall tenements on either side fearsome
to look up at—that 'The Isle of Man Arms,'
one of the most noted taverns of Auld Reekie,
was situated.   Here the Cape Club members
nightly held their 'high jinks.'   In its early
days Robert Fergusson, the poet, was a
regular frequenter, along with some of the
best wits and *literati* of the city at that time.
Among them were David Herd, Alexander
Runciman, Sir Henry Raeburn, and the
notorious housebreaker, Deacon Brodie.   At
the head of Craig's Close in 1759 a menagerie
had its abode.   A dromedary and a camel
were exhibited there, to the astonished inhabitants of Edinburgh !   According to the Press
of that time, 'they were deemed to be the
two wonders of the world, and it was doubted
whether there were other two such animals
in the whole of Great Britain !'   Paradoxical
it may seem, but 'wild animals' in those
'good old days' could hardly be called a
novelty, if the 'ongauns' of the Cape Club
roysterers, as chronicled, are to be taken as
authentic !

Another howff that had a great vogue in its

day was Fortune's Tavern in the Old Stamp
Office Close, which had formerly been the
town mansion of the Earl of Eglintoune.
The *élite* of Edinburgh, as well as common
citizens, forgathered at this place, and the
Royal Commissioner for the General Assembly
held his levees here. Poets, scholars, and
philosophers flitted from room to room, vying
with each other in paying homage to the
reigning beauties of the time. Many clubs
met at Fortune's—'The Caledonian,' 'The
Auld Herioters,' 'The Auld Watsoners,' and
'The Oddfellows.' One can imagine

> The feast of reason and the flow of soul

there must have been when such luminaries
as Hume, Robertson, Blair, and Adam
Ferguson, all members of 'The Poker Club,'
met around the social board.

Lucky Middlemass's tavern in the Cowgate,
so graphically described by the Canongate
poet in guid braid Scots, was another favourite
howff:

> When big as burns the gutters rin,
> If ye hae catched a drookit skin,
> To Lucky Middlemist's loup in,
>   And sit fu' snug,
> Ower oysters and a drap o' gin,
>   Or haddock lug !

When auld Saunt Giles, at aught o'clock,
Gars merchant loons their shoppies lock,
There we adjourn wi' hearty fouk
        To birl our bodles,
And get wherewi' to crack our joke,
        And clear our noddles!

We are very doubtful as to the clearing of noddles, with a menu of raw oysters and porter, or brandy and rum-punch, which were indulged in without restraint by the ladies and gentlemen who nightly frequented those cellars.

Other well-known howffs were the 'Pious Club,' where decent citizens met every night in a pie-house; 'The Bear Club,' 'The Wig Club,' 'The Skull Club'—the members of which drank their liquor out of a human skull; and 'The Dirty Club,' none of whom was allowed to appear with clean linen!

Bohemians our ancestors undoubtedly were, but it seems almost incredible that the beautiful Duchess of Gordon and other Scottish ladies would condescend to leave their mansions for the *laigh* shops, to partake of a plebeian feast, served upon a coarse table, in a miserable room lighted by tallow candles! The formalities of society, we are told, were thrown to the winds for the time being. Sallies, the merriest and wittiest, and remarks and jokes which elsewhere would have been considered coarse, were here sanctified by the oddity of the scene, and appreciated in the highest degree by the most dignified and refined.

All the howffs where our convivial fore-fathers forgathered have been swept away, but the eccentricities of douce citizens at that time will ever remain green in the memories of many.

JOHN HOPE'S 'WATER RATS.'

RECENTLY it was my good fortune to witness in Princes Street a striking march-past of the Edinburgh Boys' Brigade. At the Conservative Club, Sir William Lowrie Sleigh took the salute. The sight was not only an inspiring one, but recalled fond memories of the 'guid auld days.'

What Auld Reekie laddie has not had an eager desire to become a soldier-hero in his time? As a garrison city the capital of Scotland stands second to none. From time immemorial the outstanding feature has been the Castle—the famous old fortress which had bulked so largely in Scottish history for a thousand years and more.

Within the memory of many living what stirring scenes have been enacted and love of country shown, as to the martial strains of brass bands and pipers the gallant 'Forty-twa' and other Highland regiments have marched from the parade-ground, down the historic Lawnmarket, to entrain for active service. Little wonder, then, that patriotism was contagious among the Edinburgh boys. To accept the 'Queen's shilling' and fight for one's country was a laudable ambition, and recruiting sergeants profited thereby.

Veterans still to the fore have many 'tall' stories to tell of the Lawnmarket rendezvous, and of the famous recruiting sergeants, old and young Torry Gunn. The elder Torry's boast was that he had recruited half of the British Army! In spite of his cleverness, the humour of the situation was that he had enlisted many a man with a wooden leg. Years ago I numbered among my acquaintances a crony with an artificial arm, who proudly confessed that he took the 'Queen's shilling' and 'diddled' Torry Gunn twice.

I have to confess that I always had a great liking for the 'sodgers,' but I never attempted to take the 'Queen's shilling.' I can claim, however, that at a very youthful age I had the courage to present myself at the British

League, Rose Street, in order to enlist in John Hope's 'Water Rats.' Dear old John Hope! In spite of his eccentricities he was a power for good as far as the boys of Auld Reekie were concerned—the pioneer, I should say, of the present-day wonderful organisation, the Boys' Brigade.

Visions of appearing in all the glory of a red garibaldi, blue knickers, leggings, with a carbine on my shoulder, had whetted my appetite to become a Cadet. Having got my schedule filled up, which stated that I neither smoked nor drank, I presented myself at the old drill-room in Rose Street under the present Music Hall. The instructor, an old army sergeant, eyed me critically before he spoke. At length he said, 'Man, man, ye'll never be a sodger—ye're far ower jimp (small)! Gang awa' hame and tak' mair parritch!' My fate was thus sealed as regards becoming one of 'the awkward squad' in John Hope's Cadets. The standard height for recruits was 4 ft. 6 in., and at that time I was two inches short!

Boy-like, this did not damp my enthusiasm nor prevent me from being keenly interested in the 'Water Rats.' Many of the High Street and Lawnmarket boys had joined the corps, and, although too short in stature, I was kept well posted as to when a 'turn-out' was to take place.

If my memory serves me right, the little army was started in 1860. The great work of John Hope and his generosity of heart are still remembered. Nothing remains but a 'memory.' Nevertheless for many years the laddies of Auld Reekie were weekly taught and disciplined, which ultimately fitted them to become respected citizens in every quarter of the globe. What boy was not delighted to be associated with the flute or brass band, or to rise from 'the awkward squad' to the proud position of lieutenant? The first bandmaster was a Mr Parkinson, who had been in the army, and the practice-room was in Dr Bell's School, at the foot of Niddry Street.

John Hope's band did not fail to receive recognition. It turned out at the review in honour of the marriage of the Prince of Wales (later King Edward) on 10th March 1863. After the review the kindly founder invited the members of the band to his house in Moray Place, where a happy evening was spent. John was as sprightly as the boys. He joined in the singing, and danced round the table, jingling the money in his pocket, suggestive of 'I've plenty to spare!'

Nor was he unmindful of favours received

by the Cadets from the City Fathers. He instructed his officers to march the whole regiment of boys to every Town Councillor's house, where they drew up in line and presented arms, while the band played 'God Save the Queen!' A similar compliment to-day might well be paid by the Boys' Brigade to our worthy Lord Provost and Councillor Leonard Bilton, who take such a keen interest on their behalf.

On several occasions the 'Water Rats' acted as guard of honour at Holyrood, and marched in procession behind the Commissioner. They were also present at the laying of the foundation-stone of the new Royal Infirmary, when King Edward was Prince of Wales. Nor must the reviews and sham fights in the Queen's Park be forgotten. What memorable days for the boys! Fighting alongside the 'Old Fogies' and Volunteer battalions from every part of Scotland! Forming a square to resist an attack from the Fife Light Horse! The glorious charge that was made by the 'Wee Warriors!' And the capture of the enemy's guns at St Anthony's Well! What 'guid auld days'!

In 1860, the boys of the South Side, particularly in the Pleasance district, joined up in a recruiting-room in Rankeillor Street.

On a spare piece of vacant ground near St Leonard's Street they drilled two nights a week, and the drill-instructor was an old corporal of the 78th Highlanders. Another place in the Old Town where they drilled was St John's Parish Church Hall, Victoria Street, under Sergeants Dick and Elliot, of the 26th Cameronians. These instructors were strict disciplinarians. The prizes for regular attendance at drill consisted of one pair of good strong boots for thirty marks, the full attendance being sixty marks. Some boys had the satisfaction of winning two pairs of boots with the full sixty marks!

Auld Reekie has been favoured in her generous-hearted men. John Hope stands out prominently as one who in his day and generation proved a philanthropist in the truest sense of the word. From an educational point of view he did yeoman service to the community. The needy were not forgotten. Night-schools were opened throughout the city, and at Canonmills the defaulters were called the 'Stockaree mutineers!' Another night-school (George Heriot's) was in 'Society,' at Bristo Port, and Mr Martin was the teacher.

Many citizens owe their success in life to the training, both morally and physically, they received in John Hope's 'Water Rats.' Like the Auld Herioters, there must be thousands of the once 'Wee Warriors' still alive, and this may bring back happy memories of things that happened in Auld Reekie fifty years ago.

THEATRES AND ACTORS OF BYGONE DAYS.

THE Scottish Capital stands second to none in its historic associations, its 'characters,' and its drama. Long before the days of our grandfathers the Edinburgh stage held an honourable position as a purveyor of wholesome plays, which are now sadly lacking.

It is a far cry from the present day to 1736, when Allan Ramsay erected a theatre in Carrubber's Close, and in this twentieth century it must have been gratifying to all lovers of the Temple of Thespis to see a revival of that author's immortal pastoral 'The Gentle Shepherd.' The old Playhouse Close in the Canongate, however, must ever be regarded as the cradle of the legitimate drama in Auld Reekie. The theatre was erected in 1746, by John Ryan, a London

actor, but, previous to this, from 1727 till
1753, the Tailors' Hall in the Cowgate was
occupied occasionally by strolling players.

Tailors' Hall, Cowgate.

In 1768 Royal letters-patent were obtained
by David Ross to build a theatre where the
General Post Office now stands.   Previous

to this a small theatre in the Canongate was managed by the same enterprising Mr Ross amid many difficulties. The new theatre, facing the green slopes of Multree's Hill, the site of the Register House, was opened in December 1769, at a cost of £5000, and the house, when full, held £140. The lessee's troubles began with the fall of the North Bridge, which cut off almost the only safe communication with the Old Town, where the douce citizens resided. There was no New Town of Edinburgh in those days, and, as we are told, 'only a straggling house or two at wide intervals.'

Ross lost heart after a couple of unsuccessful seasons, and the theatre was leased to the celebrated actor, Samuel Foote. The appearance of Mrs Siddons at the Shakespeare house later on broke all previous records. The stony hearts of the Auld Reekie play-goers were electrified by the power of this actress, and so great was the demand for seats that vast crowds gathered at noon, many travelling from England—no easy matter in those days —to see the performance. Others 'lay all night in the streets on mats and palliasses, in order that they might get an early chance of reaching the box-office next day ; while the gallery doors had to be guarded by detachments of military, and their bayonets did not remain unacquainted with blood!'

From 1794 to 1809 this playhouse was in a very struggling condition. At that time Mr Henry Siddons, the only son of the great tragedienne, took possession of the theatre, and two of the assignee's sponsors were Henry Mackenzie, author of *The Man of Feeling*, and Walter Scott, both of whom were deeply interested in the drama. Unfortunately, in 1815 Mr Siddons died through overwork and anxiety, and during the next four years, in spite of performances by Edmund Kean, the elder Matthews, and Mr and Mrs Charles Kemble, the Theatre Royal in Shakespeare Square did not prosper.

Another financial crisis had arisen, and the big and generous-hearted Walter Scott then came to the rescue. On the 15th of February 1819 'Rob Roy' was produced. The national spirit of the play delighted rich and poor, and with actors and actresses like Hamerton as Rob Roy, Mrs Renaud as Helen Macgregor, Duff as the Dougal Cratur, Miss Nicol as Mattie, Murray as Captain Thornton, and old Mackay as the Bailie, an instantaneous success was assured. Other Waverley dramas followed in quick succession, and the financial worries of the 'treasury' were at an end.

With satisfaction I recall that my grand-father not only assisted in the painting of the scenery, but acted in many of the minor parts at the old house at the foot of the North Bridge.

In the 'fifties Mr R. H. Wyndham, a name with which Edinburgh theatres are still honourably associated, became lessee in conjunction with his talented wife. Long the greatest and most popular of theatrical managers in Auld Reekie, they continued at the Shakespeare Square house until it was demolished in 1859 to make room for the erection of the new General Post Office. For ninety years the old Theatre Royal had passed through many vicissitudes, and on the night of the 25th of May 1859, when the curtain was rung down for the last time, play-actors such as Edmund Glover, E. D. Lyons, Mr Saker, and Henry Irving, all of whom took part in the final performances of Tom Taylor's and Charles Reade's comedy, 'Masks and Faces,' and the Irish farce, 'His Last Legs,' must have left the famous house with pangs of regret.

Of the Adelphi, at the corner of Broughton, Wyndham became manager for the second time. After a series of fires it was re-opened in 1876 as the Theatre Royal. Many notable actors and actresses have trod the boards of this house, which for almost three-quarters of a century and under many names was the scene of circus, concert, and opera performances.

Present-day play-goers will still remember the triumphs of Mrs Bernard Beere as Peg Woffington, and it may interest many to know that when Walter Hatton was manager, Mrs Arncliffe-Sennett, founder and president of the Northern Federation for Woman's Suffrage, played lead with that fine actor, Barry Sullivan, at the Royal in 1887, under the stage name of Mary Kingsley, her principal parts then being Lady Macbeth and Ophelia.

The Haymarket Company, with Madge Robertson as Galatea, in Gilbert's 'Pygmalion and Galatea,' can never be forgotten.

As a tragedian, Henry Talbot, son of Calvert, a teacher in the High School, scored a great success. Talbot, unfortunately, fell upon evil times, and became in his closing years teacher of elocution in Glasgow. Sothern as Dundreary was another great favourite.

But it is as 'the house of pantomime' that the Royal will ever be remembered. What a treat was always in store for the Auld Reekie laddies, many of whom have now

bald pows and gray beards! The 'dame' of
R. S. Pillans, with his topical song in praise
of 'Oor Auld Reekie,' and many others, never
failed to become popular with the 'gods':

> Mr Abanazar, he rode upon a razor,
> A' the way frae Fisherrow, sir,
> Cock-a-doodle-do!

Many still sigh for a return of those days
of the gorgeous transformation scene, followed
by clown, pantaloon, harlequin, and columbine,
instead of the twice-nightly 'hotch-potch'
that is served up now.

Patrons from Giles' and Connor's gaff,
tatterdemalions from the Cowgate, the Canongate, and High Street, when they grew
up in years, doubtless transferred their foot-
light affections to the south side of the
city. Who can ever forget that popular little
house, the old Princess's in Nicolson Street,
and the feast of good things that the stock
company nightly produced? What boy of
the 'seventies does not remember the narrow
passage in Hill Place that gave entrance to
the gallery, and the 'sair banes' that were felt
next day after a night in the theatre? Who,
also, does not remember the boy whose cry
between the acts, 'Lemonade, gingerbeer,
spice, or oranges wanted?' never failed to ex-

tract the last coppers from the pockets of the
humble 'gods'? What a sweet mouthful was

High School Wynd.

that out of the 'twirlie poke' to the gallery
frequenters in those dear auld days! What

a galaxy of capable actors and actresses trod
the boards of the old Princess's at that time.
A. D. M'Neil, the lessee, and great Edinburgh
favourite, who gave an impersonation of Rob
Roy which has never been surpassed; George
Fisher, as the Bailie, a fine Scots actor, who
toured the world three times, but latterly fell
on evil days, and died in a lodging-house in
the Canongate of Auld Reekie; Rod Meddli-
cotte and Frank Hill. Others were Charlotte
Morley, Fred Hastings, leading heavy, Harry
Siddons, and Christie Miller, a local favourite,
who had a small shop in the Pleasance and
played Dougal in 'Rob Roy,' and was an
admirable harlequin. There also appeared at
the old Princess's J. K. Emmett, who introduced that once popular song, 'Schneider,
How You Vas?' Minnie Palmer in 'My
Sweetheart,' Walter Bentley, and Sothern as
Dundreary. The Carri Opera Company,
also, were a big draw at this house.

For years the old Princess's was noted for
melodrama, and the writer can vividly recall many of the stock actors and actresses
who were the darlings of the 'gods.' Here
Wilson Barrett and Miss Heath produced
'Elfinella,' by Ross Neil, in the 'seventies,
but it never attained a dramatic success.
Under the pseudonym of Ross Neil, Isabella

Harwood wrote many novels and plays of high merit, though too purely literary for the stage.

Here also Walter Bentley made his first appearance after his secession from the Lyceum Theatre Company, London. He was the son of the Rev. Dr Begg, the well-known minister of Newington Free Church. Bentley, after many successes, eventually forsook the stage, and took up evangelistic work in America. Who can ever forget Fred Gould as the hero, and Tom Sennet as the villain, in 'Belphegor the Mountebank,' or when they played in 'The Ticket-of-Leave Man' and 'The Dumb Man of Manchester'? How true to nature were the old men's parts of Mr Morton as 'Melton Moss,' and Mr Owen in 'Rob Roy.' Beloved by the whole 'profession,' Mr Morton lived to a good old age, and latterly was a regular attender on Saturday nights at the Carrubber's Close Gospel temperance meetings. He died in Edinburgh, and was buried by sorrowing friends in Newington Kirkyard. The actresses at the old Princess's, under Mr M'Neil's régime, could hardly have been excelled in the parts they played. They were, to mention only a few, Blanche Ford, the wife of Tom Sennett; Lottie Harcourt, wife of Harry Siddons;

Carrie Lee, Lizzie Wilmore, and Charlotte
Morley.

The New Edinburgh Theatre, now used as
the Synod Hall, and substantially built by
Sir James Gowans, was opened by Wybert
Reeve on 20th December 1875. It had a
short-lived existence, in spite of the fact that
the cast included that great Auld Reekie
favourite, R. S. Pillans. Charles Matthews
made his last appearance in Edinburgh at
this house, playing in 'My Awful Dad,' his
own comedy. The building became the
centre of the old U.P. Church, and subsequently one of Edinburgh's most com-
modious public halls.

The Royal Lyceum, in Grindlay Street,
and only a stone-throw away from the
unfortunate New Edinburgh Theatre, was
erected in 1883, and had a memorable opening
on the 10th of September by Henry Irving
and Ellen Terry. Irving had worked hard,
and was now at the top of the tree. My
friend, Mr William Fowler, of Selkirk, claims
to have been the first to pay to enter
the pit on the opening night. He is also
proud, and justly so, of still being the
possessor of a copy of the programme. I can
also claim to have been present on the opening night as a 'gallery boy.' I also possess

the programmes of the first and second week.
It was a twelve-nights' engagement, and I am
proud to record the fact that on the second
week I was present on seven occasions, which
included the matinee. So much for my
theatrical enthusiasm in the late Victorian era!

I can still clearly remember the great
crowds that flocked to Grindlay Street, and
the histrionic triumphs of Henry Irving and
Miss Ellen Terry in 'Much Ado About
Nothing,' 'Hamlet,' and 'The Belle's Strata-
gem,' the great actor playing Doricourt, and
Miss Terry, Letitia Hardy. In 'The Bells,'
the hushed audience, when Irving, as Mathias,
the Polish Jew, under the influence of the
mesmerist in the court scene, reacted the
crime, was one never to be forgotten. And
what enthusiasm at the fall of the curtain!
Following Henry Irving's and Miss Terry's
visit, the engagements included Miss Ada
Cavendish, J. L. Toole, Miss Wallis, Miss
Kate Vaughan, Ristori, Miss Genevieve Ward,
Salvini, J. B. Howard, Wilson Barrett, and
the Christmas pantomime of 'Red Riding
Hood.'

A personal incident in connection with a
return visit of the great tragedian in October
1888 may be mentioned. Appreciative verses
I had written on Irving's Mephistopheles in

'Faust' appeared in the *Scotsman*, and the following day a kind letter of invitation came from the actor, who desired my acquaintance. The meeting took place in one of the dressing-rooms of the Lyceum, and many reminiscences of his early struggles in Auld Reekie, when performing at the old Theatre Royal in Shakespeare Square, were told. I shall never forget the kindly voice and fatherly advice of the great man as to what books a young poet aspiring to fame should carefully read. He strongly recommended the British essayists, poets, and dramatists. Macaulay's *History*, Bailey's *Festus*—'a glorious magazine of ideas, glittering with fancy, and luminous with mental splendour!' as Irving dramatically put it. 'Dryden is a master it would be well to study; while Pope is always acute and logical in his writings. Read also,' he said, 'Blair's *Lectures on Rhetoric and Belles Lettres*. In biographical history study Plutarch's *Lives*, and do not forget *Don Quixote*, Rabelais, and Tupper's *Proverbial Philosophy*.' Irving spoke with enthusiasm of Auld Reekie and his many friends there, particularly Dr Pryde; of his early days when he used to climb Arthur's Seat, to study his humble part, and the great attraction the historic capital of Scotland always had for his imagination. We parted; and after the long period of thirty-eight years, that memorable meeting with the great tragedian remains as plainly in my memory as on the night we met.

It was also my good fortune to meet Miss Ellen Terry. I was accompanied by a young and aspiring playwright; the interview took place in the Edinburgh Hotel, Princes Street, the premises of which are now occupied by Rentons' Limited. My friend had brought a bunch of heather to present to the great actress. Her gracious acceptance and charming manner called forth the remark, 'Miss Terry, you are really an angel—an angel without wings!' Her smile was sufficient to show her appreciation of my friend's words, but she sweetly replied, 'A pretty compliment, indeed.' Dear old Ellen Terry!

THE GAIETY AND ITS 'STARS.'

ADMIRERS of Sir Walter Scott need not be told that the great novelist was born on 15th August 1771 at the head of College Wynd, Edinburgh, a narrow alley leading from the Cowgate to the College. Almost at the very spot where the 'Wizard' first saw the light, there still remains a place of entertainment now almost exclusively given over to picture-shows, and it may safely be said that, like many of the intelligent citizens of Auld Reekie, not one in a hundred of its frequenters knows of the historic associations so near at hand.

What changes have come about in the variety world since 1875! This little place of entertainment was once a noted music-hall, which laid the foundation of the fortune that has built so many magnificent theatres throughout the country.

'The Gaiety,' as it was then called, was opened by 'The Hall Company, Ltd.,' on the 5th of July 1875. Its early days were not auspicious, but, there came on the scene a young man who soon made his name. With that indomitable pluck and business capacity that never failed him through life Harry Moss took over the place. It was on the 24th of December 1877 that Mr Moss entered upon his lesseeship of the Gaiety. I can well remember the afternoon before the opening night, and how, along with the new proprietor, I paid a visit to a broker's shop in the Potter-row to purchase a second-hand lock and bar, and afterwards helped him to fasten it to the dilapidated entrance door of the Chambers Street Theatre of Varieties.

In his endeavour to elevate the standard of the music-hall performance, after the opening night on Christmas Eve, Mr Moss found himself virtually faced with ruin. His efforts to supply a clean entertainment did not appeal to many of the old patrons of the hall, and for weeks the performers sang to half-empty benches. It is not necessary to dwell further on the struggles and financial difficulties that beset the new lessee at the beginning of his venture. By dogged determination they were eventually overcome, and a purified atmosphere prevailed at the 'Moss Varieties.' It may interest many to recall the names of the performers who appeared on the opening night under H. E. Moss's managership: Bradley's Burlesque Waxworks, Pashur Nimrod, Madame Zonti, Graham and M'Bride, The Warriners, Misses Sandford and Smith, and J. Pollard.

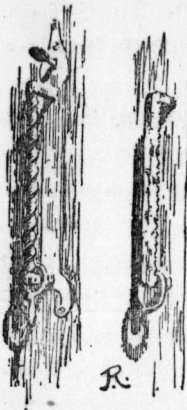

Old Risps.

Mr Moss quickly realised that bumper houses could be brought about only by strengthening what had always been a very mediocre programme. It was a bold step to

take, and a daring bid for fortune, but he was
confident that, if a London 'star' could be
brought to Edinburgh every week, it would
satisfy not only the regular patrons, but
induce many others to patronise his establishment. This innovation was speedily instituted, the result being that, in spite of their
scruples, respectable folk at last found their
way into the 'Varieties,' and, having once got
them inside, Harry Moss, with that true
business instinct that never failed him in after
life, knew enough to be able to bring them
back. The best talent of London was secured
for the Chambers Street 'house,' at salaries
ranging from £30 to £50 for the week, with
an occasional Friday-night benefit to the
'star.' The programme usually consisted of
four artistes and 'the top o' the bill,' the
contract being that the performers were to
appear twice nightly, before and after the
'star,' who appeared at nine o'clock and sang
from five to eight songs!

The venture was an instantaneous success,
and this is not to be wondered at when
vocalists like Tom Maclagan and Frederick
Maccabe, of 'Begone, Dull Care' renown,
were booked to appear. Singers with the
reputation of George Leybourne, the 'Lion
Comique,' journeyed specially from the great

Metropolis to fulfil an engagement at the unpretentious little hall in Chambers Street. Crowded houses nightly gave this artiste, deservedly popular in his day, a warm welcome, and the chorus of 'Champagne Charlie' was whistled and sung by every errand-boy. Dan Leno, who at the height of his career earned a fabulous salary, was engaged by Mr Moss to appear at the Gaiety for £8; while Lottie Collins, who sang into a world-wide popularity 'Ta-ra-ra-boom-de-ay,' was paid £6 for a week. In later years this artiste commanded three figures. Jenny Hill, the 'Vital Spark,' was another great draw.

By the flitting of his goods and gear from his abode in St Patrick Square to a villa in Minto Street, Newington, it was now evident to many that Harry Moss was making money. It was in this snug house, at a supper-party given by Mr Moss, that I first met Arthur Roberts, then handsome and slim, and one of the first favourites with the old Gaiety gallery-boys. All his songs were very popular in their day, and many will remember 'I'm going to do without 'em, don't want them any more.' The 'money-making' prediction of Moss's friends was amply verified, for within two years he was in a position to purchase the entire block of buildings, comprising the theatre, the University Hotel, and several shops, for the sum of £15,000.

About this time G. H. Macdermott was creating a furore in London with his great Jingo song, 'We don't want to fight, but, by Jingo, if we do!' Mr Moss lost no time in bringing to his music-hall the comique who had suddenly bounded into popularity. The great Macdermott's fame had preceded him, and hundreds nightly were unable to gain admission to the Chambers Street house.

> We don't want to fight, but, by Jingo, if we do,
> We've got the ships, we've got the men, we've
>   got the money too;
> We've fought the Bear before, and while we're
>   Britons true,
> The Russians shall not have Constantinople!

This 'number' drew forth rounds of applause, and Macdermott's striking appearance on the stage added to the effect of his rendering of the great war-song. Another 'star' who merited the Gaiety patrons' approval was Charles Godfrey, 'The Masher King.' His 'Girls from the School at the End of the Street' was a catchy number; but this paled into insignificance compared with 'On Guard,' a fine song-scena that always aroused the patriotic enthusiasm of the audience.

Here upon guard am I, ready to do or die,
Fighting for queen and country too, fighting for
    home so dear ;
Cannons they are in sight, bayonets to left and right ;
Hands true and steady are willing and ready,
    And hearts that have no fear.

No sketch of the old Gaiety would be
complete without a reference to W. J. Ash-
croft, the Irish comedian. For many years
this artiste delighted young and old with
his characteristic impersonations, and even to
this day the chorus of 'The Solid Man' is
occasionally heard :

Go wid me, and I 'll trate ye dacent,
    I 'll set ye down, and I 'll fill yer can ;
As I walk the street each man I meet
    Says, ' There goes Muldoon, he 's a solid man ! '

Recollections of many others still linger in
my memory—Charlie Oswald, ' The Laugh-
ing Philosopher,' whose ' Sweet Seventeen '
proved a great hit :

Sweet seventeen, sweet seventeen,
Lovely Matilda, the fairest I 've seen ;
Cheeks like the rose, eyes black as sloes,
How I love Matilda nobody knows !

Fred Coyne ; Tommy Barret, ' The Nobleman's son ' ; Fred Albert ; Tom Bowling,
Motto Vocalist ; and last, but not least,

Charles Coburn, 'The Man who Broke the Bank at Monte Carlo'!

War and rumours of war at that time had stirred up the people, and one of the first to voice the feelings of our nation in a patriotic ditty was N. C. Bostock. A native of Auld Reekie, he gained his first success in a travelling booth in the Lothian Road, where the Caledonian Goods Station now stands, the ground at that time being occupied by a circus, penny gaffs, and other shows. The fleshers of Fountainbridge claimed Bostock as their very own, and to a man they turned out nightly to hear their favourite Scots comedian sing in his own forceful and inimitable way about 'Coal Jock' or the bravery of 'The Royal Dalkeith Militia'! Bostock's 'turn' at the Gaiety was a popular one, and his singing, in immaculate evening dress, 'That's what the People Say in England,' was vociferously applauded by gallery, pit, promenade, and stalls:

> There's money in the country, and there's thunder
>   in the air;
> Little Turkey's threatened by the great big Russian
>   Bear;
> But the British Lion's watching, so she'd better
>   have a care—
>   That's what the people say in England.

Other favourite Scots comedians who appeared at the 'Moss Varieties' in the early days were Packy Fairley, J. C. Macdonald, and Harry Linn, who belonged to Leith. Simple words like the following:

> I love the lassies, the bonnie bonnie lassies,
>   I love the lassies, short or tall;
> Whether dark or fair be the colour of their hair,
>   I love the bonnie lassies, bless them all,

wedded to simple airs, quickly caught on. Other great favourites were 'Jock M'Graw, the Fattest Man in the Forty-Twa,' 'Bonnie Jeanie Deans,' and 'The Cottage where Burns was born.'

Harry Linn was a prolific song-writer; many of Sir Harry Lauder's latter-day ditties seem to re-echo those once so successfully given by Linn. Then practically unknown, the greatest of all Scottish comedians was making strenuous efforts to sing himself into public favour. As an instance of his struggle, I, along with others in connection with a series of entertainments held during the winter months in St Mary Street Hall, succeeded in bringing Harry Lauder from the west to sing at one of our Saturday evening concerts for 7s. 6d.! Out of this magnificent(?) sum, the great little comedian, who has been known to receive over £1000 a week, had to pay his own railway fare from Glasgow. It is worth while recording the fact that in 1899 Harry Lauder appeared at one of the W. & R. Chambers's employees' soirees and concerts in the Oddfellows' Hall, Edinburgh. His name was three times on the programme, and he sang six songs, one of them being 'My wee Ruggy Duggy.' His fee on that occasion was something like two guineas!

In running the Gaiety, Mr Moss had the able assistance of a relative by marriage, Mr Leonard B. Bramwell, a gentleman beloved by not only the artistes but the patrons. Once a year Mr Bramwell took a well-deserved benefit, and local talent on that night got every opportunity to prove its ability. It was on one of these occasions that Ted Watson captivated the audience with his patriotic song in praise of 'The Highland Brigade' and 'I'm Saving it all for Mary.'

Hurrah for the Kilties, brave lads every one,
Of foemen they're never afraid ;
Like the hills of their native land, firmly they
    always stand,
The pride of old Scotland, the Highland Brigade !

Other 'locals' who gave promise of distinguishing themselves were Sam and Harry

Irvine and Peter M'Kernan, all clog-dancers,
clog-dancing being much in vogue then.
Many Edinburgh lads drifted into the 'profession,' and M'Kernan, journeying to England to dance for the championship of the
world, was defeated by only one point by
J. H. Haslam.

Compared with present-time music-hall performances, it must be confessed that many
items in the olden days, particularly the
specialty act 'turns,' have been greatly improved upon. In every line of the 'business,'
with the exception of the 'star,' this has been
very noticeable; and it goes without saying
that many of the songs then inflicted on a
not too critical audience would not be toler-
ated now. In recognition of the part he
played in the elevation of the music-hall
entertainment, King Edward conferred on
H. E. Moss, in December 1905, the honour
of knighthood. It was well deserved, for
the struggles and successes of this great
music-hall pioneer read like a romance.

Palatial variety-palaces abound in every
city in the empire to-day, and, looking back
on the 'guid auld times,' I have a feeling of
conscious pride as one closely identified with
my old friend, Sir Edward Moss, when he
first began.

THE AULD KIRKYARDS.

IT would take a volume to record the virtues and the failings of some of the notable dead in a few of Edinburgh's old kirkyards. The antiquarian and the bookworm are fully conversant with the life-history of these men and women, who in their day and generation trod the plainstanes of Auld Reekie, and added undying lustre to the names they bore. Nowadays, however, with so much of the ' deil-tak'-the-hin'maist ' policy, and frivolous pleasure in vogue, it has to be confessed, with regret, that many, old and young, know little or nothing of Edinburgh's illustrious dead.

Greyfriars Kirkyard has been aptly described as the 'Westminster of Scotland.' As far back as 1562, the Magistrates of Edinburgh made an application to Maria R. for the ground. To present-day readers the quaint words of the appeal may be interesting :

' Becaus our said toun is populous, and the multitude thairof great, that your Hienes will gif to us the zairdis of the Grayfreiris and situation thairof, being sumquhat distant fra our toun, to mak ane burial place to burie and eird the personis deceissand thairin, sua

that thair-trow the air within oure said toun
may be the maire puire and clene.'

To this petition the queen readily gave
her consent.

Of the illustrious dead, records show that
George Buchanan, the humanist, historian and
poet, was the first
man of note to
be buried in the
kirkyard. He
died in 1582,
aged seventy-six,
in Kennedy's
Close — long
since swept
away — which
stood near the
Tron. It seems
strange that the
burial - place of
this noted man
of letters is not
known, although
we are told 'his
funeral was at-

Monument in Greyfriars.

tended by a great company of admirers.'

A few yards from the entrance, and on a
bit of raised ground, the curious-minded may
find the stone on which, legend alleges, the

National Covenant was signed on the 28th of February 1638. In defence of the Church against the aggressive measures of Charles I., five thousand persons, including the future Marquis of Montrose and many peers, put their names to the parchment, before 'a mighty concourse, who, with uplifted hands, weeping eyes, and drawn swords,' were determined to shed their life's-blood for the religious liberty of Scotland's Church.

Passing many strangely-sculptured stones, we move down the brae to 'that grim memorial of suffering, tears, and blood,' the Martyrs' Monument:

> The tomb that tells of men so true:
> The martyr'd Marquis!—Guthrie, brave!
> And Renwick, wha would be nae slave!
> Wi' ithers of the fearless dead
> Wha for King Charles had little dread,
> But focht against tyrannic laws,
> For God, their conscience, and a cause!
> And prov'd Christ's Crown and Covenant
> To be nae idle, reel-rall rant!

From 1661 to 1688, eighteen thousand, including the Marquis of Argyll, were either murdered or destroyed for the glorious Cause, and buried here!

What Auld Reekie laddie half a century ago did not hear from his 'faither or mither'

the story of 'Bluidy Mackenzie,' and tales
of the 'ongauns' of the resurrectionists in

'Bluidy Mackenzie's' Tomb.

bygone days? Sir George Mackenzie was
so abhorred as a legal persecutor after his

appointment as a King's Advocate in 1677
that his ghost was supposed to haunt the
place where he lies in Greyfriars Kirkyard. The old days of superstition are gone,
and, viewed in the light of the present time,
it must be confessed that 'Bluidy Mackenzie'
proved a most illustrious ornament to the
College of Justice by his remarkable sagacity
and distinguished eloquence. As the founder
of the Advocates' Library Sir George's name
will live for all time.

Lovers of 'the gude auld Doric'—and their
names are legion in spite of the pessimists—
still direct their footsteps to the spot where
'the mortal part of an immortal poet' lies.
As the author of *The Gentle Shepherd*, it can
be claimed for Allan Ramsay that he gave
to the world one of the finest pastorals in
British literature.

> Tho' here you 're buried, worthy Allan,
> We 'll ne'er forget ye, canty callan';
> For, while your soul lives in the sky,
> Your 'Gentle Shepherd' ne'er can die!'

Ramsay wrote many poems in the Scottish
vernacular, including that fine old lyric,
'Lochaber No More.' But 'honest Allan'
was more than a poet. He not only carried
on a successful wig-making business in the

High Street of Edinburgh, but set up a cir-
culating library, and attempted to establish a
theatre in Carrubber's Close at a time when
the play-house was looked upon with much
disfavour. Ramsay was born in 1686, and
died in 1758, and in a commanding position
in Princes Street gardens, at the foot of the
Mound, a full-length marble statue from the
chisel of Sir John Steell commemorates the
poet's worth.

In this old and much-frequented city of
the dead lie the remains of many a douce
citizen in his day and generation. Walter
Scott, the father of the great Sir Walter;
George Heriot, father of ' Jinglin' Geordie';
Willie Creech, Provost of Edinburgh in 1811,
and the well-known publisher of the works
of Burns. By the poet he was immortalised
in the following racy lines:

> O, Willie was a witty wight,
> And had o' things an unco sleight;
> Auld Reekie aye he keepit tight,
>   And trig and braw,
> But now they 'll busk her like a fright—
>   Willie's awa' !

It is recorded that ' Willie' was ' gey
sweer't to pairt wi' the siller,' and on various
occasions he and Burns were at loggerheads

'ower the settlin' o' accounts' long overdue
the bard.

John Porteous, captain of the Old City
Guard, who met his fate at the hands of a
Grassmarket mob in 1736; and John Kay,
the celebrated engraver, whose portraits of
noted Edinburgh citizens are still much
sought after and valued by the antiquaries,
also lie buried in the Greyfriars Kirkyard.

Quitting this 'God's acre,' with its hallowed
memories of the past, we halt for a moment
at the head of the Candlemaker Row.

What Auld Reekie laddie does not know
'Greyfriars Bobby,' the neat little granite
memorial drinking-fountain which commemorates the simple incident of a Skye
terrier's devotion to its dead master? In
1871 it was my good fortune to see 'Bobby'
one day in Traill's Coffee House, in Greyfriars Place, and to give this much-loved
animal a half of a buttered 'bap.' 'Bobby's'
master, a Midlothian farmer, named Gray,
who had been in the habit of calling at the
coffee-house on market days, along with his
canine companion, suddenly died, and was
buried in Greyfriars Kirkyard. Three days
later, at the usual hour, 'Bobby,' hungry and
'sair bedraigled wi' the rain,' made his appearance at the old howff. 'I kent the beastie,'

Mr Traill once said to me, 'and he no sooner got something to eat than he bolted away. For nearly a week the same thing happened, then I began to wonder, syne made up my mind to watch where the doggie gaed to.' The kindly Mr Traill soon discovered that the faithful animal had returned to the Greyfriars Kirkyard. Every effort to induce 'Bobby' to take up his abode in the diningrooms failed, although he was a regular daily visitor when the one o'clock time-gun was fired from the Castle. For nine years, night and day, in summer or in winter, the little Skye terrier kept watch over its dead master's grave. 'Bobby' died in 1872, and was buried in Greyfriars Kirkyard, and it was through the generosity of the late Baroness Burdett-Coutts that the drinking-fountain at the head of Candlemaker Row was erected to perpetuate the memory of 'Greyfriars Bobby,' a faithful dog she once saw.

Leaving that last resting-place of many notable dead, we wend our way along Bristo to the old Chapel-of-Ease. Here in this sombre and never visited kirkyard lie the remains of Dr Adam, rector of the Royal High School. Thrift propaganda is much in evidence to-day, and it might be interesting to recall the frugal fare of this great teacher when he was a lad attending the University. 'He lodged in a small room at Restalrig, for which he paid fourpence per week. His breakfast consisted of oatmeal porridge with small beer; his dinner often of a penny loaf and a drink of water. Yet at the age of nineteen, so high were his attainments, he obtained—after a competitive examination— the head-mastership of Watson's Hospital.' Dr Thomas Blacklock—the blind poet who, in 1786, so enthusiastically proclaimed the genius of Burns to the *literati* of Edinburgh as to induce the Ayrshire bard to visit the Scottish capital, and publish the first Edinburgh edition of his poems—is also buried here.

Another whose name will go down to posterity, and who was laid to rest in Buccleuch Kirkyard in 1795, is Mrs Cockburn, the poetess, who wrote the modern version of that immortal lament, 'The Flowers o' the Forest.'

I 've seen the smiling o' fortune beguiling,
  I 've tasted her pleasures and felt her decay ;
Sweet was her blessing, and kind her caressing,
  But now they are fled, they are fled far away.

Near to the last resting-place of Mrs Cockburn was buried Deacon Brodie, the housebreaker, after being hanged at the head of Libberton's Wynd. He is supposed to have been the prototype of Robert Louis Stevenson's *Dr Jekyll and Mr Hyde*.

Let us now wend our way to the Canongate, and enter its old kirkyard. Across the greensward, there, closely built against the back of the Old Tolbooth, is the tombstone of a provost of whom Auld Reekie should ever feel proud. Sir George Drummond was born in 1687. He was with Argyll's forces at Sheriffmuir, and fought at the battle of Prestonpans. Six times Lord Provost of Edinburgh, he was also founder of the Royal Infirmary, and laid the foundation stone of the old North Bridge. He died in 1766, leaving a record which would be difficult to surpass.

Not many yards away stands the simple stone erected by Robert Burns to 'a brither bard.' As well as the Ayrshire ploughman might every Scot 'uncover his head,' for there was laid the wasted body of Robert Fergusson, the youthful poet.

> This humble tribute with a tear he gives ;
> A brother bard, he can no more bestow ;
> But dear to fame thy song immortal lives,
> A nobler monument than Art can show.

So wrote the sorrowing Robert Burns. Another Robert—Robert Louis Stevenson—

has often paid homage to his 'earlier brither in the muse.' In a letter he says: 'When your hand is in it, remember our poor Edinburgh Robin. Surely there is more to be gleaned about Fergusson, and surely it is high time the task was set about.' Luckily, this has been ably done by A. B. Grosart in the 'Famous Scots' series.

At the foot of the kirkyard a tall granite monument, erected by the generosity of Mr Ford in memory of the soldiers who died in Edinburgh Castle, situated in the parish of Canongate, and interred here from 1692 to 1880, arrests the eye.

> Their country's sons will around this stone
>   Oft speak of the deeds of the brave,
> And gratefully look on the grassy sod
>   That grows o'er the soldier's grave.

A few yards away, Horatius Bonar, the great Scottish divine, lies buried. His theological works were numerous, but he will be best remembered as the author of the simple hymn, 'I heard the voice of Jesus say, "Come unto Me and rest."'

Admirers of our national bard have doubtless often moralised over the 'Clarinda affair.' Mrs M'Lehose, whose maiden name was Agnes Craig, was born in Glasgow in 1759.

Deserted by her husband, she settled in Edinburgh in 1782, and in 1787 made the acquaintance of Robert Burns. She was then twenty-eight, cultured, good-looking, and possessed of no mean poetic gifts. At their very first meeting there sprang up a strong mutual attraction. Burns did not hesitate to declare: 'Of all God's creatures I ever could approach in the beaten way of friendship, you struck me with the deepest, the strongest, the most permanent impression.' Then followed his much-discussed 'Letters to Clarinda.'

Until her dying day Mrs M'Lehose fondly cherished the memory of the poet, and, as the inspirer of 'Ae Fond Kiss' and 'My Nanny O,' her name will live along with the immortals. She lived to a ripe old age (over eighty), and was here laid to rest in 1841. For years the spot could with difficulty be located, but by the efforts of one of the Edinburgh Burns Clubs a tablet, with a striking medallion of 'Clarinda' in the centre, was some time ago placed in the wall, near where she was buried. The memorial was unveiled by Mr Joseph Laing Waugh at an impressive ceremony in the Canongate Kirkyard.

Another literary celebrity buried in the Canongate Kirkyard is John Ballantyne, the publisher, and for a long period the intimate friend of Sir Walter Scott. The disastrous business connection with the Ballantynes is well known, but this did not prevent the big-hearted romancer from paying his last respects to the dead along with Lockhart, on the 16th of June 1821. 'I feel,' whispered Scott in his son-in-law's ear, 'as if there would be less sunshine for me from this day henceforth.' This sympathetic remark was characteristic of the great 'Wizard.'

A handsome mausoleum records the worth and philanthropy of Sir William Fettes, twice Lord Provost of Edinburgh, and founder of that great educational institution, Fettes College. Here also was laid Adam Smith, author of *The Wealth of Nations*, a book that has been the source of much mental inspiration. The vault of Dugald Stewart, philosopher, and friend of Burns, is situated near the foot of the brae. In his house in the Horse Wynd, in his day, he entertained many distinguished guests, including Lord Palmerston. The Ayrshire poet, who was frequently in Stewart's company during his stay in the Scottish capital, summed up the professor's character, divided into ten parts, thus : 'Four parts Socrates, four parts Nathaniel, and two parts Shakespeare's

Brutus.' What would the world not give to-day to behold the professor and the poet taking their morning walk, as was their wont, to the Braid Hills, to look 'from Nature up to Nature's God'?

Of the others whose mortal remains lie here may be mentioned Alexander Runciman, the well-known historical painter, and George Chalmers, the founder of Chalmers' Hospital. It is also supposed that the body of ill-fated David Rizzio was interred in the Canongate Kirkyard. Much research, however, has failed to confirm this traditional story.

Many others whose names were once a household word lie buried in this old kirkyard, which, like Greyfriars and Buccleuch, is teeming with memories of a glorious past.

BYGONE PANTOMIMES.

WHAT changes the whirligig of Time has brought about!

> The happy auld days noo awa',
> Fu' dear they were to us a';
> Tho' often we fret, we should never forget
> The happy auld days noo awa'.

With the advent of Christmas, memories of auld cronies whose friendship I enjoyed around the festive board, and the entertainments then in vogue, are often recalled. Christmas and New Year in Auld Reekie were sombre affairs compared with the present day.

Entertainments at that time were on a limited scale, and undoubtedly the pantomime season was eagerly looked forward to by young and old. Carnivals, variety-theatres, Palais-de-Danses, and palatial picture-houses were unthought of. At the Theatre Royal London 'stars' for many months in the year drew the intellectual patrons; and at the Princess's, in Nicolson Street, the stock company produced national and melodramatic plays, a revival of which would undoubtedly be of a more educative nature than the 'problem' monstrosities of the present day.

And what triumphs of stagecraft and acting were the pantomimes produced at the Broughton and South Side playhouses in the 'sixties, 'seventies, and 'eighties! What haunting 'numbers' and topical songs were always sung. Some of the choruses remain in my memory even to the present day. And what popular favourites were most of the artistes! Many of Auld Reekie's citizens now 'hirplin' doon the brae' still recall with enthusiasm and flashing eyes the grand old 'mummers' who never failed to delight them in the days of their youth.

As the 'home of pantomime,' first place must be given to the Theatre Royal, under the Howard and Wyndham régime.

In 1868 the first pantomime produced was 'The Butterflies' Ball.' This was followed by 'Saint George and the Dragon,' in which Fisher, the pantomime favourite, scored a great 'hit' with his song commemorating a whale stranded in the Forth, which became famous as the 'Longniddry Whale':

> 'Twas in the year of '69,
>   October the 20th day,
> That a mighty whale swam up the Forth,
>   As big as the Isle of May.
>   Brave boys!
> And when this monster they secured,
>   By the tail and round the snout,
> 'Twas then they found a baby whale,
>   And his mother didn't know he was out.

From this song the catch-phrase emanated, 'Does your mother know you're out?'

'Goody Two Shoes,' 'The House that Jack Built,' 'Old Mother Hubbard,' and 'Blue Beard,' drew the crowds to the Broughton Street 'house.' In 'Blue Beard,' topical allusions to the St Mary's Loch water scheme gave the comedians many oppor-

tunities to score; while the report of Dr
Livingstone's discovery of the source of the
Nile was responsible for the following:

> Oh Doctor, in your travels, pray list to me awhile,
> > Sweevalink tum tum;
> Did you ever come across the source of the Nile?
> > Sweevalink tum tum.
> I was told by the man who keeps the light upon
> Inchkeith,
> > Sweevalink tum piro si,
> That the source of the Nile was the Water of Leith,
> > Sweevalink tum tum.

Another song which became very popular
was:

> > If ever I cease to love,
> > If ever I cease to love,
> > > May the camels have the mumps
> > > On the top of their humps,
> > If ever I cease to love.

Frank Hill as Blue Beard, George Fisher
as a nondescript Scoto-Mussulman, Lizzie
Wilmore as Fatima, Carrie Lee as Selim,
took a verse each of this topical number.
It quickly caught on, and was whistled and
sung in every home.

In the mid-Victorian period many pantomimes surpassing those of the present day
were annually produced. What a treat was
always in store for the bairns half a century

ago! What spectacular triumphs were 'Red Riding Hood,' and 'Aladdin,' with Maggie Cooper as Aladdin, and 'Cinderella'! No pantomime at the Royal was complete without the 'dame' of R. S. Pillans, with his topical songs. One in praise of 'Oor Auld Reekie' became immensely popular:

> A braw, braw toon is oor Auld Reekie,
> A thrifty toon is oor Auld Reekie;
> The a'e toon's modern, the ither antique-ie,
> A wonderful toon is oor Auld Reekie.

'Keep it dark,' 'That's what puzzles the Quaker,' and 'Jim the Carter Lad' were very popular ditties half a century ago.

'Spice, lemonade, and oranges!' was a familiar gallery-cry in the Royal at pantomime time. I wonder how many of the citizens of Auld Reekie are still alive who remember Tam Cochrane (a pipe-maker to trade), who supplied the 'gods' with the palatable refreshments; also the magnificent glass chandelier which hung from the ceiling of the auditorium, and unfortunately perished in the great fire? It was the admiration of every patron. Many frequenters of the Royal in the 'eighties must sigh for a return of the gorgeous transformation-scene, followed by the comic business of the clown, pantaloon, harlequin, and columbine. Who could ever forget Persivanni, the great clown, and Saker as pantaloon?

'Puss in Boots' takes my memory back to the days of the old Princess's, when that successful pantomime was first produced at the Nicolson Street house. Allan Thomas, with his drolleries as the 'King of Cockalorum,' Neish and Martin as 'Peasemeal' and 'Soordook,' Sydney Lewis as 'The Fat Boy' ('Wake up, Joseph!'), and many others in the cast must have gladdened the heart of the lessee, the late Mr A. D. M'Neil. No one was more capable of judging of a good thing, and he never failed to please his patrons with excellent Christmas and New Year fare.

Like myself, some may still remember the stirring declamation of the 'King of Cockalorum':

A singular thing in pantomime to do,
Ere the King speaks, is to bash a head or two:
I'll not be troubled with condescensional rot,
But, striking out a new line, I'll—bash the lot!
    I'm King of Cockalorum!

At the close of the pantomime, as is customary with present-day favourites, Allan Thomas's benefit always meant a packed 'house,' the Freemasons of the Edinburgh Lodges turning out in large numbers.

'Bo-Peep' was also another very successful
pantomime at the old Princess's, and, if my
memory does not play me false, Miss Lizzie
Wilmore played the principal part as Little
Bo-Peep; Mr Lester, the granny; Miss
Lester, the fairy queen; Mr Hill, Pompey;
Mr Delewar, Father Time; and Mr Clive, the
Dragon. They were all good theatrical stuff
in their day.

Of all the pantomimes produced by Mr
M'Neil, first place, however, must be given to
'The Babes in the Wood.' From first to last
it was a triumphant success. It ran for
months at the old Princess's, and had to be
withdrawn only to make room for other 'book-
ings.' Not only was the 'book' a palpable
hit, but the tuneful melodies and 'business'
of the comedians still haunt the memories of
those who heard them. And what a galaxy
of artistes! Brown and Newlands as the
ruffians, Allan Thomas as the wicked 'uncle,'
the Misses Minnie and Dot Mario, to mention
but a few of the company.

Notwithstanding its great success, pantomime was afterwards discontinued at the old
Princess's, and light opera took its place, such
as 'Les Cloches de Corneville,' with Miss
Florence St John, Cora Stuart, Mr Bedford,
and Shiel Barry as 'Gaspard.' Another famous

actress to appear at the Princess's was Miss
Kate Santley, with Mr Sydney Harcott, in
'La Mascotte.'

A counter-attraction to the old Princess's
was the Southminster, also in Nicolson Street,
where the present Moss's Empire now stands.
Levy was the lessee, and this place of
entertainment occasionally staged a play of
the melodrama type, and the house was
familiarly known as 'The Soothie.' Although
there was no music-hall opposition, it never
proved a paying concern. The large interior,
with its dirty and rain-bedraggled ochre-
stained walls, was always cold and uninviting.
Nevertheless, many good artistes in their own
particular line of business appeared at this
house. I can recall Ben Hoskins, who sang
into popular favour a ditty that is heard to
the present day:

> Lang may we live to praise
> Scotland's bonnie woods and braes.
> Ye'll maybe think I'm gaun ower far, but I like to
> blaw my horn;
> For education and intellect
> We bang the world in that respect—
> As fac' as death I'm glad to think that I'm a
> Scotchman born.

A 'life' of fifty years is not bad for such
a doggerel song. Others who appeared at

the Southminster were those famous heroes
of the ring, Jem Mace, then in the zenith of
his fame as a pugilist, and Poly Mace.   They
gave a capital boxing exhibition, also a living
statuary 'turn,' which included 'Apollo,'
'Ajax Defying the Lightning,' and 'The
Dying Gladiator.'

A few years ago I had a talk with Jem
Mace in one of the side-shows of the Waverley
Market Carnival.   The eyes of the old veteran,
then hale and hearty, brightened when a few
incidents of bygone times in Auld Reekie's
Southminster were recalled to his memory.
'Ay, lad,' he said, with a friendly grasp of the
hand and a quiver in his voice, 'them were
the good old days indeed !'

Most, if not all, of the 'mummers' who
delighted us in the days of our youth must
have passed away, but their efforts to amuse
at the festive season will ever remain a
happy memory to many of the citizens still
alive in Auld Reekie.

SOME FAMOUS SINGERS.

AS a member of the Edinburgh Pen and
Pencil Club it was my good fortune
to be present at one of their Burns Nights
in the month of January.   Scots songs and

recitations, particularly those of our National Bard, chiefly made up the programme. What impressed me most, however, were the remarks made by Mr Robert Burnett, the eminent vocalist, regarding Scots songs, and the eulogium he paid to those singers who, by their natural rendering and simplicity of vocalisation, proved their artistry in the singing of the auld Scots sangs.

Reminiscences of a few singers whose names were household words in Auld Reekie half a century ago were vividly recalled—men and women who, in their day and generation, thrilled the hearts of large audiences. Memories of bonnie Scotland, its patriotism, glens, heath-clad hills, and bonnie lassies, were awakened. John Templeton, John Wilson, and David Kennedy were a notable trio.

The name of John Templeton will ever be remembered by those who have made a study of the lives of great singers. From being a young precentor in Rose Street Secession Church, Edinburgh, he eventually succeeded in taking the London stage by storm, a feat as difficult to accomplish in those days as it is at the present time.

Templeton came to Edinburgh at the age of twelve. At sixteen he was advised to give up singing, owing to his voice changing.

During the next four years he continued to study music, and at twenty he became precentor. His fame spread as a singer and teacher, and in spite of 'warning voices' he resolved to take the plunge in a theatrical career.

Crossing the Border, Templeton's first theatrical engagement was at Worthing, in Sussex. In this town he performed for three weeks without salary, but the young tenor had confidence in his abilities, and with hard study his reputation increased. He next appeared at Brighton, and crowds flocked to hear him. Templeton had now captured the hearts of English audiences, and he was offered and accepted an engagement as first tenor in the Southampton and Portsmouth Opera Company. His success resulted in an offer from the lessee of Drury Lane.

At Covent Garden, Templeton also scored a great success in 'Don Giovanni.' Begrez, the distinguished tenor, who had been studying the score for eight weeks, suddenly gave up the part. The opera was to be produced a week later, and the lessees were in desperation. Templeton was approached, and, after much hesitation, he agreed to fill the gap. Five days for the preparation of such a part as Don Ottavio is probably unrivalled in operatic history. The young Scotsman was an instantaneous success, and after the first night he had London at his feet.

In the year 1843 Templeton turned his attention to recitals and Scottish song. His 'Nicht wi' Burns' and 'The Rose, the Shamrock, and the Thistle' were mostly carried through by himself. Wherever he went, in Great Britain, Ireland, and America, he swayed the hearts of the people, and, being careful with the siller, when he died he left a fortune of over £80,000. Surely not an insignificant sum to have accumulated in 'the guid auld days.'

At the age of fifty Templeton retired from the profession which for over thirty years he had so conspicuously adorned. His retiral into private life, however, did not affect the generosity of his heart. On several occasions he again appeared on the concert-hall platform, and sang, with as much acceptance as before, several of his most popular songs for charitable objects. In his old age this great Scotsman was a familiar figure in London, and revered by all who knew him. His death in 1886, in his eighty-fourth year, was deeply regretted by the whole of Europe, but more particularly by his own countrymen at home and abroad, who were proud of the illustrious

Scot, who by his unequalled rendering had popularised so many of the auld Scots sangs.

Auld Reekie has every reason to be proud of John Wilson, who was born in the Canongate on Christmas Day 1800.   At the age of

Canongate.

ten he was apprenticed to the printing firm of Walker & Greig, and shortly afterwards at Paul's Work entered the employment of James Ballantyne, who at that time was issuing from his press the Waverley Novels.

Wilson's beautiful voice quickly attracted attention, and, when free from the exacting duties of proof-reading, he devoted his spare time to the theory of music and vocal exercises.

Wilson became a member of the choir of Duddingston Church, from which he secured a precentorship in Roxburgh Place Relief Church. His fame as a singer was quickly recognised, and concert engagements in rapid succession followed. In 1825 he was appointed precentor in St Mary's Established Church, and, leaving the printing trade for good, he devoted his whole time to the teaching of music. In spite of his success, John Wilson seized the opportunity of further improving his voice, by studying under Lanza, in London; and under Crivelli and Aspull, who were masters in the art of voice-production in their day.

In 1830 Wilson resolved to give up precenting, and become a public singer. In the same year he made his first appearance on the stage of the old Theatre Royal as Harry Bertram in 'Guy Mannering.' Sir Walter Scott was present on that occasion, and complimented the singer. I have a justifiable pride in saying that my grandfather appeared along with John Wilson on the stage of the Shakespeare house on that memorable night.

Shortly afterwards a tempting offer from the Covent Garden management was accepted, and the Canongate laddie joined his brother Scot, Templeton, in London. These now world-renowned artistes sang in many operas and at concerts in London with unparalleled success. Eight years later the indomitable Wilson crossed the Atlantic, and not only took America by storm, but made a fortune. Four years later he had the honour of singing his Scottish songs to young Queen Victoria during her visit to Taymouth Castle, to the great delight of Her Majesty.

At the request of his many overseas admirers Wilson again crossed the Atlantic in 1849, a fateful journey to the famous Scottish singer. In Canada, where his 'Jacobite Entertainments' drew crowded houses, his career was suddenly brought to a close. At Quebec he had gone on a fishing expedition, and contracted a chill through being soaked with rain. Cholera was raging at the time, and in his weakened state he caught the infection. He died within a few hours, on the 8th of July 1849, in his forty-ninth year. Those who were privileged to hear John Wilson sing, and well qualified to judge, have declared that his remarkable voice, which was of great compass and pure tenor quality, if once heard could never be forgotten.

To come to a later period, well within the memory of many still alive, David Kennedy will be remembered as long as people love to sing the songs of Scotland.

Although not a native of Auld Reekie, Kennedy dearly loved 'mine own romantic town,' for it was there he undoubtedly first got his foot on the bottom rung of the ladder of success by his interpretation of the auld Scots sangs.   Born at Perth in 1825, he came of a singing stock, for his father was precentor of the North United Secessional Church in that city.   His uncle, too, was a precentor; and young Kennedy had excelled so much in music that before the age of twenty he frequently officiated as precentor for both his father and his uncle in their respective churches in Perth.   The fame of John Templeton and John Wilson spurred the young house-painter to higher things, and to the eternal credit of the former, when Kennedy gave his first four concerts in the old Hanover Rooms, London, the once great tenor was present at each of them, and congratulated the singer on his artistry and vocalisation.   Migrating to Edinburgh, Kennedy received music lessons from Edmond Edmonds, a well-known music-teacher in his day. A year later he received an appointment as precentor in Nicolson Street United Presbyterian Church. Having abandoned his trade, he removed to Edinburgh, and took up his abode in Nicolson Street, opposite the church.

In spite of his musical abilities, Kennedy, like many another genius, did not escape the struggle of having to find bread and butter for his wife and young family at the beginning of his career. To eke out a livelihood he became a teacher, and gave an occasional concert in Edinburgh and the surrounding districts.

Slowly but surely, however, the young Scot was making a name for himself. Having now resolved to devote his whole attention to the concert platform, he was engaged to appear at the Burns Centenary, which was held at St George's Hall, Liverpool, in 1859. Kennedy's success was instantaneous, and any doubts as to the wisdom of his decision to become a public singer were set at rest. That same year he gave twelve successful concerts in the Buccleuch Hall, Edinburgh. Among those who took a keen interest in the singer's future were Professor Aytoun, William and Robert Chambers, the publishers, and many other distinguished citizens.

After an extended tour in Scotland in 1862–63, David Kennedy for the second time visited London. This was a risky experiment, but with that inborn confidence in the power of Scottish Song, he gave a series of a hundred concerts in the Egyptian Hall, Piccadilly, with great financial success. Although it can hardly be said that the mantle of Templeton or of Wilson had fallen on Kennedy, nevertheless his name and fame spread throughout the habitable globe. In 1864–65 Kennedy's family joined their father in the concert-hall business, and for many years shared the honours that were showered upon him both at home and abroad. It was while on tour, and when visiting Canada, that David Kennedy, to his credit, thoughtfully arranged for the proper upkeep in all time coming of the monument in Quebec to John Wilson, the famous tenor and Canongate laddie, whose untimely death deprived Europe of a prince of song. Jealousy in the 'profession' was a negligible quantity in the 'guid auld days.'

One of the most tragic events in the life of any singer happened to David Kennedy in 1881. Three of his talented family, Kate, Lizzie, and James, were on their way to study

under Lamperti, a famous Italian professor.
Breaking the journey at Nice, they went to
the new Théâtre des Italiens to hear a new
opera by Verdi. During the performance
the theatre took fire, and along with many
others they perished in the flames. David
Kennedy was abroad at the time, but his son
Robert, who was in this country, hurried to
Nice, and could identify only one of the
bodies. Such an irreparable loss few enter-
tainers, if any, ever experienced before, and the
blow to David Kennedy was one from which
he did not quickly recover. On his return
to the concert-hall platform it was evident
that his great loss was shared by sympathetic
audiences wherever he went.

Kennedy's song-recitals in the Music Hall,
Edinburgh, always drew crowded and enthusi-
astic audiences. Gifted with that pawky
mother-wit, on the platform as well as in
private life, he rendered the auld Scots sangs
in a way that could never beforgotten.

I can still recall his singing of ' The Barrin'
o' the Door,' and his vivid interpretation of
the poet's meaning, which he conveyed to
his hearers by his gestures on the platform.
Kennedy not only sang the songs but acted
them as well, to the intense delight of the
audience. This great exponent of Scottish

song died while on tour at Ontario, and his
remains were brought to Edinburgh and laid
in the Grange Cemetery. Kennedy's death
removed one whose place as an interpreter
of the humorous songs of Scotland, so far,
has never been filled. It may be worth while
mentioning the fact that a stone with medallion
portraits of Templeton, Wilson, and Kennedy
was some years ago placed on a rock at the
steps leading to the Calton Hill.

The present generation owe a debt of
gratitude to a number of vocalists who
followed in the footsteps of David Kennedy.
Patriotic to the core, and imbued with a love
for their native land, by their power of voice
they did much for the Mother Country in
cementing the bond of friendship with our
kith and kin across the sea.

No one did more to bring about this desired effect than Jessie Maclachlan, one of
the queens of Scottish song, who was born
at Oban. In 1900 this Highland singer's
name was a household word at home and
abroad. Possessing a sweet, powerful voice
and great dramatic ability, she sang herself
into the hearts of the people by her rendering
of such songs as 'Cam' Ye by Athol,'
'Whistle and I'll come to Ye,' and 'The
Hundred Pipers and A'.' At the request of

many admirers, in 1904–5, Jessie Maclachlan,
along with a select concert party, embarked
on two lengthy tours abroad. The first
covered a period of seven months, and almost
every town in Canada and America was
visited, including the trip through the
Rockies to Vancouver. The second tour
was even more successful than the first, some
of the countries visited being Australia, New
Zealand, *via* Honolulu and Fiji. This trip
extended to sixteen months, and evoked great
enthusiasm from the exiled Scot for the
songs of the homeland. Connected with the
party was Douglas Young, a tenor vocalist,
and an Auld Reekie laddie. His duets, 'The
Crookit Bawbee,' and 'When Ye Gang Awa',
Jamie,' in conjunction with Jessie Maclachlan,
proved the artistry of the singers, and never
failed to move the audience to enthusiasm
or tears. With a passionate love for the
songs of Scotland, Douglas Young resusci-
tated many gems that might have sunk into
oblivion; Allan Ramsay's 'The Lass o'
Patie's Mill' being an example.

Mention must be made of other singers
who in the 'seventies and 'eighties were very
popular on the Edinburgh concert-hall platform. When I was a boy Helen Kirk was
much in evidence in 'My Nannie's Awa','

Eliza Hunter was another great favourite. Other worthy exponents of Scottish songs were W. H. Darling, Tom Walker, James Galloway, William Crawford, R. P. Jennings, and James Lumsden, whose singing of Jamie Smith's 'Auld Edinburgh Cries' never failed to meet with much appreciation.

To-day a great Scottish tenor is much to the front. Edinburgh may well feel proud of Joseph Hislop, for he is another Auld Reekie laddie. His success in Milan and elsewhere as an operatic artiste must have cheered the hearts of his many admirers. We are all proud of Hislop, and I trust that in his wanderings abroad he 'winna forsake the auld Scots sangs.'

A PRINTER POET AND THE PENNY-GAFFS.

THE story of Old Edinburgh is to a large extent bound up in our nation's history, and it behoves us, as far as possible, to keep green the memory of the worthy citizens of Auld Reekie, who in their day and generation played no unworthy part. No apology is required for giving a brief sketch of one of the most versatile of Scotland's minor poets.

James Smith was born in a tumble-down tenement in St Mary's Wynd in 1824, and his school-days were few. At the age of eleven he was apprenticed to a printer in a small office adjoining. As a journeyman compositor he worked in Scotland and Ireland, and was employed for a time as a reader on the *Scotsman*, through which channel some of his most popular verses, including 'Burd Ailie' and 'Wee Joukydaidles,' appeared.

In 1869 he was appointed librarian of the Mechanics' Library, a post which he held until his death. He died in Edinburgh in 1887, and was buried in the Grange Cemetery, where a handsome monument, raised by public subscription, commemorates his worth. In later years his spare time was mostly spent in writing Scottish sketches for a well-known Glasgow weekly.

In 1866 Smith gave to the world *Poems, Songs, and Ballads*, which immediately established his reputation as one of the foremost of Scotland's minor poets. The book ran through several editions, and several of the songs were set to music, and became popular numbers on the concert-hall programmes. In

'Burd Ailie' we have a successful imitation
of the old ballad:

> Burd Ailie sat doun by the wimplin' burn,
>   Wi' the red, red rose in her hair;
> An' bricht was the glance o' her bonnie black e'e,
>   As her heart throbb'd fast an' sair.
> An' aye as she look'd on ilk clear wee wave,
>   She murmur'd her true luve's name,
> An' sigh'd when she thocht on the distant sea,
>   An' the ship sae far frae hame!

while his bairnhood verses such as 'Clap,
Clap, Handies,' 'Baloo, My Bairnie,' and 'Wee
Joukydaidles,' have never been equalled.

> Wee Joukydaidles, toddlin' out an' in:
> Oh but she's a cuttie, makin' sic a din!
> Aye sae fou' o' mischief, an' minds na what I say:
> My very heart gangs lowp, lowp, fifty times a-day!
> Wee Joukydaidles—oh my heart it's broke!
> She's torn my braw new wincey to mak' a dolly's
>   frock.
> There's the goblet owre the fire! The jaud! she
>   weel may rin!
> No' a tattie ready yet, an' faither comin' in!

It is to be regretted that Smith's 'Edinburgh Cries,' which had a great vogue in its
day, and which the late James Lumsden
rendered so successfully, has also been con-
signed to the limbo of the forgotten. In

six characteristic verses the song gives a true
picture of the street-vendors in Auld Reekie
half a century ago, and the ' cries ' that were
then so familiar to every citizen:

> Loud the cries are ringin', ringin',
>   Cheery ringin' up an' doun ;
> Short but sweet the sang that 's singin'
>   Blithely through Auld Reekie's toun.
> Wandrin' weary, wet or dry,
> Hark yon sonsy maiden's cry—
> ' Four bunch a penny, the bonnie caller radishes ! '
>   *Oh they 're bonnie, come and see them,*
>   *Taste an' try before ye buy.*

In his volume of verse, many of the poems
show a burning hatred of the oppressor and
his sympathy for the poor :

> An' the factor stood before her, wi' his scornfu' greedy
>   e'e ;
>   An' the bluidhounds o' the Roupin' Cross were
>   stannin' i' the stair ;
> An' he ask'd for what he kent fu' weel the widow
>   couldna gie,
> Sae he harl'd her bits o' things awa—a waefu' sicht
>   to see ;
>   An' she wrung her wither'd hands in despair.

A patriot to the core, he never tired of
extolling the land of his birth, and the heroes
whose names are enshrined in Scottish history.

His pathos has drawn tears from many an eye, particularly in 'The Wee Pair o' Shoon' and 'Wearin' Hame.' His language is never forced or artificial.

In his later years James Smith devoted the most of his spare time to writing fiction. His *Wee Curly*, *Mistress M'Larty's Second Man*, and *Pate the Penter*, published in serial form, greatly increased the circulation of a Glasgow weekly, and made the writer's name a household word at home and abroad. The stories were full of unbounded Scots 'wut' and rollicking humour. His appreciation of what was droll and homely in Scottish character was genuine, keen, and penetrating. Previous to this he had published a number of books suitable for Scots readings, such as *Peggy Pinkerton's Recollections* and *Jenny Blair's Maunderings*.

Smith was ever ready to give his services for a deserving object, and I can still vividly remember him holding spellbound an audience that filled the Music Hall, George Street, while he was on the platform giving one of his inimitable sketches. In Auld Reekie there must still be many who in the 'eighties were convulsed with laughter as they sat and listened to him discourse on 'Tibbieleerie on Scandal,' with no make-up except a handkerchief tied round his head to represent an auld wife's mutch, and his reiterated catch-phrase, 'Eh, but I hate scandal!'

It was my good fortune to know Jamie Smith for many years before he died. One of my pleasantest recollections is that afternoon in the summer of 1881, when, along with Robert Louis Stevenson, I visited some of the old closes in the Royal Mile, and took my literary companion to Riddle's Close in the Lawnmarket, and introduced him to the printer-poet, who was then acting as librarian to the Mechanics' Library, in the famous old mansion of Bailie Macmorran.

At his bedside in Parkside Street, a few days before he died, Smith recalled this incident as well as another. That was the night when Smith's *Wee Curly*, which had been 'dramatised' by the 'gaff,' was first produced. Paying my penny, and taking my seat along with the author in the dilapidated wooden erection, with 'bated breath' I awaited the rise of the curtain. Tweedledum, one of the principal characters in the play, was played by Paddy, an Irishman from the Salt-market of Glasgow, and a 'lad o' pairts,' but, whether the Scots of the character or the 'Scotch' of an adjoining tavern was most to blame, Paddy failed for once to merit the appreciation of the none too critical 'first-nighters.' Thankful to make a hasty retreat from the evil-smelling atmosphere of the

Bailie Macmorran's House.

famous 'penny-gaff,' the author of the story returned to his home a sadder and wiser man. The 'honour' of witnessing that melodrama in Blackfriars Street, and the injunctions of the tatterdemalion audience to the actors to 'Dae it ower again, Curly!' or 'Paddy, gie's anither fa'!' are things to be remembered. Jamie Smith afterwards confessed to me that for a couple of days he was unable to leave his

Blackfriars Wynd.

house, the Blackfriars Street performance had so paralysed his brain!

Some of my happiest evenings were spent when a laddie in this temple of Thespis. And what a bill of fare! Two and three shows a night, with a change of programme every time, and legitimate melodrama at that, including 'Belpheger the Mountebank,' 'The Colleen Bawn,' 'The Polish Jew,' 'Rob Roy,' 'Cramond Brig,' 'The Ticket-of-Leave Man,' 'Sweeney Todd,' 'The Laird o' Dumbiedykes,' and occasionally a play of the immortal Shakespeare! I can still clearly remember that home of the 'legitimate,' and the cry of the impatient audience, 'Up wi' the hippen!' also the public-house next door, where the actors and actresses, I am sorry to say, frequently fortified themselves for their 'arduous rôles' by quaffing the ale and porter sold at that howff.

On the south side of the Cowgate, at the foot of the High School Yards, stood another penny-gaff, and it was there that Ned Holt occasionally appeared in the rôle of Hamlet. Poor Ned! I can still picture the Prince of Denmark, after his 'triumph' in Connor's geggie, wearily making his way to his humble abode in the White Horse Close. Many will remember this unfortunate worthy, whose water-colour sketches of Old Edinburgh characters are much sought after, and still adorn the walls of a few of the older public-houses in the city. Leaving the gaff one night after playing Hamlet, Ned made for the Tron, where he found Davie Arkley and Jamie Main, two blind street vocalists, singing at the door of the 'Crystal Palace.' Taking off his dirty cap, in a melodramatic

Davie Arkley and Jamie Main.

voice he addressed the crowd: 'Ladies and Gentlemen, the Prince of Denmark does not consider it beneath his dignity to go round

with the hat.' And round with the hat he
went, making a good collection for his brothers
in adversity. This pathetic incident came
under my own observation almost half a
century ago. Ned Holt played many parts
during his checkered career. When a boy
he was apprenticed to Wilkinson, a baker in
the Grassmarket, but the Hallow Fair booths
and penny-shows proved his undoing, and he
became a Bohemian. Ned was found dead on
the roadside one night after the Musselburgh
Races.

In his day and generation James Smith, the
printer-poet and story-writer, was a citizen of
whom Auld Reekie felt justly proud.

THE ORANGE COLOURS.

THE annual election of Captain of Orange
Colours is looked upon by many members of the Edinburgh Town Council as
something in the nature of a 'freak' appointment. Our City Fathers and the citizens
of Auld Reekie may well be forgiven if
they are unacquainted with the history of
the old Edinburgh Society of Trained Bands,
and the once high and dignified office of
Captain of Orange Colours.

Rumour has it that on all ceremonial occasions and at trades' demonstrations the Captain of Orange Colours, seated on a white charger and holding aloft the venerable flag, is expected to lead the citizens along the causeway of the historic Royal Mile. Rumour, however, is oftentimes a lying jade! The veracity of this statement can be met with an unqualified denial so far as present-day demonstrations are concerned.

I doubt if a revival of the following quaint 'march-out,' described in the Records of the Society, which took place in 1718, would appeal very much to the present generation :

'The Lord Provost road alone, ushered by two of the captains of the City Guard and several trumpets ; next road the magistrates and members of the Councell, and then the officers of the Train Bands, in maner following : The comandant by himself, with the city hout-boyes before him ; then the next four captains, after them the first four lieutenants, then the eight ensigns of the first battalion. The whole Train Band officers were well mounted, with great furniture, with sword and pistols ; and when they went down the Canongate and throu Leith, they held all their swords drawin in their hands ; and when they returned into the city, which was by the West

Port, they all drew their swords, and road with them so down the Cowgate, up Saint Mary's Wynd, and so up the High Street to the Lucken booths, opposite to Don's, where the Society of Captains were handsomely entertained by the Magistrates and Councell with a

Canongate.

splendid supur, and got a great many thanks from their colonel for the good appearance they made.'

The Trained Bands of Edinburgh were instituted in 1580, from which date they were periodically elected by the Town Council, sixteen citizens, representing the merchants and crafts, to be captains of the sixteen companies of the regiment, also one lieutenant, one ensign and two sergeants to each captain, making in all forty-eight commissioned officers and thirty-two sergeants; or a total of eighty commissioned and non-commissioned officers. The captains elected annually one of their number to be commandant, afterwards styled 'Moderator.' It would thus appear that the Edinburgh High Constables to a certain degree are following in the footsteps of their illustrious forefathers.

From documents in the archives of the Corporation it is clearly shown that as far back as the seventeenth century there was an undoubted spirit of freemasonry in the ancient Trained Bands of the city. 'From labour to refreshment' was rigidly adhered to, and the convivial ongauns in John Clerihugh's, in the 'Star and Garter' in Writers' Court, in no way detracted from the serious-minded business of those whose patriotic motives induced them to protect our old romantic town.

Here is a copy of an account rendered to the Captain of the Trained Bands after a splore in Fortune's Tontine Tavern (opposite the Guard House) in 1797 ; Supper, £6, 4s. 2d.; 46 bottles port, £8, 12s. 6d. ; 19 bottles sherry,

£3, 16s.; rum punch, £2, 13s. 6d.; whisky
tody, 2s. 6d.; brandy and gin, 9s. 6d.; porter,
7s. 6d.; negus, 5s. 6d.; beer and bread, 8s. 6d.;
biscuits, prawns, &c., 7s. 9d.; breakage, 8s.;
fruits, &c., 19s. 4d.; tea and coffie, 12s.;
cadies and paper, 3s. 6d.; rum tody, 6s.—
£25, 16s. 7d.; waitters, £1, 1s.—£26, 17s. 7d.

From the year 1607 the practice of guarding
the town by means of a hired watch prevailed
down to the year 1625, when the ancient
method of watching by the burgesses and
inhabitants was reverted to by the Magistrates
and Council by their Act of Council of 19th
October of that year. In the following year
(1626) a new watching organisation was resolved upon, owing to the foreign wars then
existing and the possibility of invasion. At
that period, it is supposed, the Trained Bands
of the city were formed. Subsequently, by
an Act dated 9th May 1645, the Council
remodelled the whole arrangements of the
Trained Bands, and in 1648 a company con-
sisting of three-score soldiers, with a lieutenant,
two sergeants, and three corporals, received
orders from the Magistrates to keep watch
over the city day and night. This company
of soldiers must have been the origin of the
regular Town Guard, who, in conjunction
with the Trained Bands of the city, were

called out in arms on all important occasions, such as the sitting of Parliament and the execution of the Marquis of Huntly.

In 1663 the Society of Captains of the Trained Bands received a constitution from the Town Council, and, under the authority granted, they formed themselves into a society, the records of which, going back to 1676, are still extant. The Minute Book of the Society, with other paraphernalia, was annually handed over for safe custody to that member of the Town Council who held for the time the office of Captain of Orange Colours.

In 1798 the Town Council, in consequence of the threatened invasion by France, and the formation of the Royal Edinburgh Volunteers, suspended the appointment of officers of Trained Bands during the pleasure of the Council. Between 1789 and 1850 there are no minutes, but the Magistrates and Council appointed, in 1848, the Captain of Orange Colours and Commandant of Trained Bands, and they continued to make this appointment annually, the Commandant at that period presenting to the Magistrates and Council, at their annual dinner, a 'riddle of claret.'

Many well-known Lord Provosts of Edinburgh, and famous citizens of their day, were Captains of Orange Colours, including Adam

Smith, author of *The Wealth of Nations*; Hugo Arnot, historian of Edinburgh; William Creech, publisher of the first Edinburgh edition of Burns's poems; Sir William Fettes, founder of Fettes Hospital; Walter Scott, grandfather or grand-uncle of Sir Walter; also Bailie Lewis, Sir James Steel, and Sir Andrew M'Donald in more recent times.

Some years ago, on the suggestion of the late Mr James Russell, principal city officer, the famous old Orange flag was suitably framed to preserve it from further decay, and a replica was procured. Both flags, along with the snuff mull, tobacco pipe, and pipe-case and silver cup of the Trained Bands, may be seen in the Corporation Museum.

Any member of the present Town Council appointed Captain of Orange Colours may well feel proud. As one who has been privileged to hold the office for several years, I trust this brief sketch will help to create a further interest in the doings of our forefathers—citizens who not only loved their native city but were loyal to King and Country.

OLD-TIME SWIMMERS.

FOR some time past it has been freely asserted that Portobello is now 'a back number'! Even the Glasgow trippers seem to have 'stawed' of the Brighton of the North, and are seeking fresh fields and pastures new. Critics have loudly denounced the Edinburgh Town Council regarding their want of vision in failing to keep up to date this once attractive seaside resort. I hold no brief for the Portobello representatives in the Town Council, but make bold to say that each and all of them have endeavoured, and are still endeavouring, to do their best for the development of the eastern suburb.

The suggestion of a new pier and an open-air bathing-pond on the foreshore recalls memories of half a century ago, when the swimmers of Auld Reekie seldom or never grumbled at the facilities afforded them for a gala in the primitive swimming baths, or a plunge in the 'briny.' My recollection goes back to the days of the old public baths that stood in Washing Green Court (now Holyrood Square), in the South Back Canongate. Who can ever forget that the boys used to scramble into the 'tubs' and paddle up and down the bath? There, when a mere 'nipper,' it was my misfortune to fall into the deep end, and, had it not been for my timely rescue by Mr James Watson, a noted swimmer in his day, these Edinburgh memories would never have been written. The Canongate baths at that time were under the supervision of Mr James Crichton, a famous swimmer and an enthusiast for competitions. Some of the crack frequenters were Mr J. Paul, Mr Andrew Henderson, Mr Dan Morrison, Mr J. Park, and Mr J. Tarbert. One of Crichton's successes was the promotion of a 300 yards handicap race, and swimmers came from all parts of the country. Glasgow sent John Cowie, half-mile champion, and London sent Sam Abbot. Both were looked upon by their admirers as certain winners. Auld Reekie at that time had many promising young swimmers, particularly Dan Morrison, who was the first among Scottish swimmers to use the overhand stroke. The Canongate baths that night were crowded to overflowing, and, after a great race, Dan Morrison, the Edinburgh man, was first, Cowie of Glasgow second, and Abbot of London third. Morrison's time was two seconds faster than the previous championship time, and he received a great ovation.

I wonder how many can remember Mr J. L. Johnstone, of latter-day Bovril fame, who at that time occupied a building in Washing Green Court for the manufacture of his essence of beef? Mr Johnstone had a shop at the corner of St John's Street, now a greengrocer's. Mr Lawson, Mr Johnstone's uncle, had the business first, and on his death John (who along with his two sisters and one brother had been brought up by Mr and Mrs Lawson) succeeded to the business. He was a great favourite with everybody. Some years later he opened the shop at West Preston Street (now Brechin Brothers); and later still gave that up and went to Canada. Johnstone's Fluid Beef was well known for some years, and was followed by Bovril (Ltd.). Mr Johnstone must have been a lover of the graceful art. He gave a gold medal, value £10, for competition at the Chain Pier, to the Forth Swimming Club and the Humane Society, for the best rescue of a drowning person. The medal was won by Mr James Crichton.

In those 'guid auld days' the Edinburgh laddies divided their attention between the Canongate baths, the Nicolson Street baths, and the Union Canal! What pleasures—and pains—were the outcome of disporting themselves in the waters of Port Hopetoun! How delightful was a long swim (in spite of an occasional mud bath) in the vicinity of Castle Mills, and, what was considered a feat in those days, the 'bridging of the Canal,' namely, swimming from one bridge to another at Slateford! Those enjoyments were not without their cares. It was common for the boys on the left bank who carried the clothes to be surprised by the sudden appearance of a constable. A shout of warning was instantly given, and, clambering out of the Canal, a dozen naked youngsters, with the fleetness of Spring-heeled Jack, would scamper across the fields and escape arrest!

After the Canongate baths were closed, most of its habitués migrated to the only other establishment in the city, Pitt Street baths, which were kept by Mr Thriepland. Mention of the old structure and of the frequent contests that took place, must revive many happy memories to many an Auld Reekie laddie. Chief among the competitors and prize-takers at that time were Joe Cowan, conversationalist, linguist, and ventriloquist; Dan Morrison, Robert Hardie, Andrew Henderson, J. Paul, James Crichton, Andrew Anderson,

James Milne, John Boyle, John Aitken, Robert Bertram, J. H. Walls, and others. All of them were a credit to their native city. Graceful swimming in those days was no innovation, and Mr J. H. Wall's breast-stroke was often admired. An improvement in exhibition - swimming has undoubtedly taken place since the days of the Pitt Street baths, and an Edinburgh lassie, Miss Jeannie Veitch, still worthily upholds the prestige of her native city—which in recent years Miss Ellen King has still further enhanced by breaking records for more than one distance.

Many worthies were associated with Mr Thriepland's baths, but no one has left a more unfading memory than 'Jamie,' the money-taker at the door. A terror to the boys in those days, nothing would induce him to drop a penny off his fourpenny charge for admission. And what old-timer does not remember how satisfying it was to be faced with newly-baked currant 'bricks' at a half-penny each, especially after a long swim, and a ravenous appetite? Lucky was the laddie who had a 'bawbee' left to purchase a currant 'brick' and satisfy his hunger.

Later on, however, a strong counter-attraction was inaugurated at the Gymnasium in Pitt Street. The ground acquired by the

promoters faced Royal Crescent, and formed
what at one time was part of old Canonmills Loch. The opening of the Gymnasium
in the late 'sixties was such a novelty that
it quickly drew the younger folks. The
unique feature of the Gymnasium was 'The
Great Sea Serpent,' a large circular boat,
on which the boys and girls derived much
enjoyment when set in motion, to the
accompaniment of the Blind Asylum Band.

Joe Cowan, long associated with Pitt
Street baths, under Mr Thriepland's management, was captain of 'The Great Sea Serpent.'
Worthily he carried out his arduous duties.
Another attraction was the introduction of
the velocipede, or 'bone-shaker' as it was
jocularly termed. I can still remember the
'sair banes' that followed after an hour's
hard labour on the primitive cycling track.
This was not to be wondered at, when the
weight of the bicycle, with its wooden wheels
and iron tires, is taken into consideration.

In spite of what cynics say, historical
associations still appeal to many. What
swimmer of the 'seventies and 'eighties does
not recall the pleasant hours spent at the
old Chain Pier, Trinity, which was erected
in 1822, and washed away by a storm in the
autumn of 1898. It was, undoubtedly, the

recruiting-place for those who favoured sea-swimming. What delightful Saturday after-noon aquatic displays were given at the end of the pier! Its destruction was deeply re-gretted by many citizens of Edinburgh and Leith. What memories those morning and afternoon 'dips' must revive, especially the feat for the learner of being able to swim to the raft, in water twenty-six feet deep at full tide! The pier was also the headquarters of the Forth Swimming Club, the pioneer of organised swimming in Edinburgh. The Lorne, the Police, the Leith, and the Eastern Clubs came later, and did yeoman service in fostering this healthy sport. The Rosebery, instituted in 1880, and the Hibernian in 1888, were fortunate in capturing some of the crack swimmers of the Chain Pier days.

What of the old brigade? It is gratifying to be able to record the fact that many of the veterans who were heroes to the boys of half a century ago are still hale and hearty. I mention a few: Mr John Aitken (the oldest member of the Lorne), Mr Dan Morrison, Mr Robert Hardie, Mr James Crichton, and Mr J. H. Walls. Long may they be spared to tell the story of their triumphs. May it be an incentive to Auld Reekie laddies and lassies of the present generation to go and do likewise, and worthily uphold the traditions of our city. I am confident an open-air swimming-pond at Joppa will soon be an accomplished fact; but a pier at Portobello will be a question for City Fathers in the 'dim and distant future.'

A NOTED DETECTIVE.

MORE than half a century ago no man was better known or more generally dreaded by the criminal classes in Edinburgh than James M'Levy.

'Jamie' was an Irishman, and proud of the country to which he belonged; and it has to be said to his credit that his tongue never forsook the brogue. The son of a small farmer in County Armagh, he migrated to Scotland at an early age, and found employment in Edinburgh with a builder and tax-surveyor. On his entering the police force in 1830 as a night watchman, his ingenuity, decision, and courage appealed so much to Captain Stewart that three years later he was appointed to the detective staff. Such as met 'Jamie' for the first time might have taken him for a well-to-do farmer from the 'Emerald Isle' on a visit to Scotland, intent on 'a deal.' He

was of medium height, square-faced, and clean
shaven, and always wore a tall silk hat, from
beneath the broad brim of which a pair of
quick black eyes scrutinised the crowd as he
sauntered along the streets accompanied by his
faithful companion Mulholland. Although
his work was mainly confined to the 'Historic
Mile'—from Castlehill to Watergate, from
every close or wynd of which he was always
ferreting out his 'bairns'—nevertheless, during
many years of activity, the New Town, as well
as the Old, received much of his attention.

It is claimed for M'Levy that during his
thirty years as a detective he investigated
almost three thousand cases, and usually got
convictions. Murders and assassinations were
not in 'Jamie's' line, his energies being confined to the common details of burglaries and
shop-liftings. Yet he was king of detectives
in Scotland in his day. How he would stand
if measured alongside some of the men who
have had to deal with the detection of crime
since his time matters very little. In the
'forties and 'fifties his name was a household
word, not only in Auld Reekie, but 'far ayont
the sea,' and memories of the stirring parts he
played still survive.

As well as detective, M'Levy during his
busy lifetime essayed the rôle of author, and

his *Curiosities of Crime* and *The Sliding Scale of Life* had a great run of popularity. In narrating his experiences he relates how detectives sometimes come off second-best, and as a typical case, showing the ingenuity of thieves and the wonderful readiness with which they will outwit the minions of the law, the story may be told of how Jean Brash, at that time one of the most noted of the thieving fraternity in Edinburgh, easily got the better of the 'force.'

This case, in which the famous detective often declared he would have scored had he been on the 'job,' was that of a young dandy with more money than sense. Promenading Princes Street one night, clad in the most expensive furs, Jean Brash, with finely-formed features, and dark hair well set off with a hat of exquisite taste, doubtless gave the 'glad eye' to that 'nut' of long ago. Entering into conversation with the most notorious thief that ever walked the streets of Auld Reekie, in a few minutes the young man discovered that a five-pound note was missing from his pocket. A constable at that moment was passing, and Jean was charged with the theft. Without more ado, the constable and the victim searched Jean carefully. Her pockets were turned out, but no five-pound

note could be found. Then they looked all
over the pavement, but nothing in the shape
of paper could the policeman's lamp discover.
The protesting Jean was then marched to the
Police Office in the High Street. In the
charge-room she was more minutely searched
by a female warder, but without success, and
still declaring her innocence in an injured tone.
The officer in charge began to have his doubts
as to the truth of the young dandy's story,
with the result that after little more than an
hour's detention the accused was set at liberty.
Shortly afterwards the daring and adroit Jean
returned to Princes Street. At the corner of
Castle Street she had not long to wait ere her
quick eye detected the policeman who had
arrested her. In a moment she was by his
side, and shook him effusively by the hand.
More than astonished at meeting the woman
he had arrested little more than two hours
before, he nervously asked, 'What's your
game now, Jean?' 'I want to tell you something in secret,' she replied. 'I'll tell you
where the five-pound note is if you'll promise
not to blab to M‘Levy. It would make a nice
present to take home to your wife.' ''Deed
ay!' answered the unsuspecting Donald. 'I
know I can trust you; but who's your tailor?'
asked Jean laughingly. 'You're makin' a fule

o' me. What has that to do wi' the siller?'
cried the constable angrily. 'Everything,
Donald,' said Jean, as she still held his arm
firmly and fumbled about the cuff of his coat.
'The tailor doesn't spare his cloth, and gives
you a deep cuff. It's as handy as a pocket.'
Thrusting her nimble fingers into the cuff of
the constable's coat, with flashing eyes she
looked him straight in the face. 'Suppose
you find the note in here after I am gone;
I'm sure you wouldn't know how it got there,
would you?' 'No,' answered the constable
excitedly. 'Then search your cuff!' cried
Jean, as she released her hold of his arm. 'It's
there—a bonny New Year's gift to take home
to your wife!' And before the constable had
time to collect himself, the woman had disappeared from his side. Full of confusion,
the man began to search, but failed to find
anything, for Jean Brash, while pretending
to put the five-pound note in the cuff, had
actually abstracted the note which she had
so cunningly placed there when about to be
marched to the police office two hours before.

Jean's favourite promenade was the Grassmarket, in those days one of the busiest
quarters in the whole of the city. During the
afternoon until nightfall, when the fair was
in full swing, crowds of young and old, full

of eager excitement, surrounded the long line
of barrows that stretched from the Bow to the
old Corn Exchange at the foot of the spacious

The West Bow.

street.   The smell from the scores of flaring
paraffin-oil lamps in no way tended to disturb
the appetites of those eagerly devouring the
toothsome gingerbread, sliced coco-nut, or

'bluidy puddin's.' The clamouring voices of the hucksters endeavouring to dispose of their wares, mingled with those of the keepers of the travelling booths, from the front of which ear-splitting music filled the air, along with the roaring of the wild animals in Wombwell's Menagerie, made the surroundings a veritable inferno. In those dear auld days the citizens of Edinburgh could not resist the temptation of spending a few hours in the Grassmarket, viewing the sights. For the youngsters the familiar cries of 'Try your luck! A penny a shot!' 'Red-cheekit apples—buy them up!' 'Rock—braw strippit rock, a bawbee the stick!' and 'Sold again; the money's paid!' had seductive attractions that only the younger generation could fully appreciate. For the older people chief interest was centred in the multifarious shows, whose inartistic bills-of-fare were closely scanned by the gaping crowd. Fastidious indeed must have been the tastes of those who could not find entertaining variety in the innumerable penny-gaffs and petrified mummy exhibitions that faced one at every turn.

The following may be taken as another sample of the many cases that passed through M'Levy's hands, cases in the investigation of which he almost invariably achieved success.

The tenant of a flat in Coates Crescent had
gone for a short holiday, leaving his house shut
up. On his return he discovered that burglars
had been busy during his absence.   Many valu-
ables were missing, and M'Levy was called in.
Having obtained a list of the stolen goods,
which included gold rings, earrings, brooches,
and silver-plate, 'Jamie' realised that he had
a difficult job in hand, as most of the articles
were suitable for the melting-pot. A small
musical-box was also missing, and this gave
M'Levy some hope of discovering the thieves.
Having been informed by the owner that one
of the tunes the instrument played was 'The
Blue Bells of Scotland,' the first step he took
was to go round the brokers and see if any of
the 'haul' had been offered to them for sale.
This had not been done. Days of fruitless
attempts to find a clue followed, and he
had almost given up the chase as hopeless.
Sauntering down Blackfriars Wynd one evening, he drew up suddenly at the door of a
public-house, for his ear had caught the sound
of a musical-box playing. He listened, and
heard the box tinkle out 'The Blue Bells of
Scotland.' Entering the howff, he was informed by the landlady that the box had
been left accidentally there by a man whom
she described. From the description, M'Levy

spotted one of his 'bairns,' and immediately proceeded to the house where he lived. After some difficulty he gained admission, for 'Jamie M'Levy's knock' was well known to every one of the inmates. At a glance he saw that he had unearthed the thieving gang. Summoning to his assistance two policemen, he searched the den, and in less than half an hour recovered nearly the whole of the stolen jewellery. The man and his companions were shortly afterwards tried and transported.

On the question of how far punishment had a tendency to diminish crime, M'Levy in his day did not hesitate to voice his opinions. He firmly believed in industrial schools rather than jails for the reformation of juvenile defaulters. During his long connection with the Criminal Investigation Department, the effects of his exertions had a marked influence on the diminution of crime in Auld Reekie. Able and shrewd, yet with a good deal of genuine humanity in his heart, he won the respect of his most bitter enemies, and actually endeared himself to such as were not fatally wedded to crime. That he ran risks, as all detectives do, goes without saying, and on several occasions he met with serious injury from his 'bairns.'

But M'Levy survived it all, and lived to a good old age, worn out more by the inactivity of retirement than by any effects of his strenuous life.

THE BODY=SNATCHERS.

MANY an Auld Reekie laddie who has reached the three-score years can, doubtless, still remember the weird stories told by his parents in his bairnhood days, when sitting at the cosy chimla-lug on eerie winter nights. Or when snell winter had taken its departure, and genial spring had clothed the trees in a mantle of green, a visit to the beauty-spots, or to the old and historic kirkyards in the vicinity of the home, will ever be remembered. In those dear days of auld langsyne week-end excursions had not come into vogue, and fortunate were the youngsters who were privileged to get farther afield than a mile frae 'sweet Edinburgh toon.'

This had its advantages as well as its drawbacks. The youthful minds in those days were more concentrated on the stirring events that had happened at their very doors, and imagination ran riot as they viewed the sombre and strongly-stanchioned vaulted tombs of the dead.

Truth was vouched for in the recital of the gruesome stories of the body-snatchers, who at one time in Edinburgh plied a lucrative trade. I can still remember the story told by my revered granny of an incident that happened in the Greyfriars Kirkyard. Despite the vigilance of watchers, who were ever on the alert, and whose duty it was at certain hours of the night to fire their muskets to scare away the resurrectionists, the ghoulish work of opening a new-made grave was begun. The body of a wealthy lady had been interred that day, and a pair of expert body-snatchers were losing no time in prising open the coffin. Their eyes were soon dazzled by the sight of a number of valuable rings on the fingers of one of the hands. A small saw was quickly taken from their bag, and the act of severing the finger commenced. To their horror the 'dead' woman sat up in her coffin, and, her shrieks of pain re-echoing as far as the Candlemaker Row, the sacrilegious pair took to their heels and managed to escape. The resurrectionists that night got the fright of their lives. As was afterwards explained, the old lady had been buried in a trance, an occurrence said to be common at a time when a doctor's certificate of death was not so essential as now.

Digging corpses out of their graves and selling them as 'subjects' to lecturers of anatomy was an almost daily occurrence during the middle of the eighteenth century. We are told that at that period, owing to the progress in the science of anatomy, and the increasing number of medical students, professors found the supply of 'subjects,' which had previously been obtained from the bodies of executed criminals, quite inadequate to meet the wants of the surgical and medical schools. When prices ranging from £8 to £10 could be obtained for a body, without inquiry being made as to how it had been procured, it is not surprising to find that during the first quarter of the nineteenth century a flourishing trade was carried on.

So daring had the resurrectionists become that, as a precaution against the ghoulish fraternity, heavy gratings were placed over new-made graves, spring-guns were set, and in many cases fully armed friends of the deceased persons night after night took their turns by the graves until the corpses could be of no service to the doctors. Nevertheless, so great was the demand for 'subjects' that grave-diggers were bribed to keep out of the way when a body was being raised.

The passing of the Anatomy Act of 1832

proved the death-knell of this risky trade. A few years previously, however, the body-snatchers of Edinburgh were very busy in this 'profession,' but more vigilance on the part of the burial authorities rendered the supply of subjects for anatomical schools almost impracticable, which resulted in the demand for dead bodies becoming greater than ever.

At length the time came when a series of crimes in Edinburgh was destined to rouse the whole of the people of Europe to horror. Recognising the risk of those who made body-snatching a regular business, with an ingenuity of device which enabled them to carry on their work for a long period with unerring success, William Burke and William Hare conceived the idea of supplying the demand for bodies without incurring the danger of being caught opening a grave. Burke was born in the county of Tyrone in 1792. After a varied career in Ireland, he landed in Scotland, and for a time worked as a labourer on the Union Canal. Having abandoned his wife in Ireland, he formed a connection with a woman, who was afterwards known as the notorious Helen M'Dougal. Reaching Edinburgh, the couple made the acquaintance of Hare and Mrs Log by becoming their lodgers. Hare's dwelling-place was known by the name of Log's Lodging-House, and was situated in the West Port. The infamous abode has long since been demolished, but I can still remember the vivid description of the place given by my mother, who was one of a crowd that raided the kitchen after the arrest of the murderers, and annexed, among other things, a three-legged pot, which is still in my possession. It was a small, self-contained dwelling of one flat, and consisted of three apartments, two of which could be readily inspected from outside by the denizens of Tanner's Close. The third room looked upon a pigsty and a dead wall at the foot of the uninviting alley. It was in this squalid lodging-house that vagrants from all parts of Scotland and Ireland found quarters for the night.

The fiendish partnership was begun in 1827; and the first exploit of the notorious pair was the sale of the body of an old pensioner who had died in Hare's house, for which they received the sum of £7, 10s. Robert Louis Stevenson in his *Picturesque Notes* alludes to Burke, sitting at a window at the Cowgate Head, watching the burials in Old Greyfriars, with the ultimate object, no doubt, of desecrating the graves. This can only be described as a bit of a myth, no evidence having been forthcoming to prove that William Burke ever attempted to resurrect the dead.

The glamour of the gold in their first transaction and the hint from the Surgeon Square doctors that more bodies would be readily taken induced the heartless pair to look out quickly for another 'subject.' Prowling in the Grassmarket on a dreary December afternoon in 1827, Hare observed an old woman under the influence of liquor. With little difficulty he induced her to accompany him to Tanner's Close. There she was introduced to Burke and the two women, and more drink was procured, but, whether through fear or because their intentions were defeated, it was not until the following day, when Abigail Simpson, their first victim, lay in a drunken stupor, that Burke and Hare fell to work and suffocated the 'lodger.' That night the body was conveyed from the West Port to Surgeon's Square, and £10 was obtained for it.

Flushed with this success, and having quickly got rid of their ill-gotten gold, the murderers, with the help of the two women as decoys, next induced a vagrant named Mary Haldane to visit the house in Tanner's Close, and a repetition of the ghastly tragedy in the little room in Log's lodging-house was

there enacted. That same night the body
was carried to the anatomists, and, to the
surprise of Burke and Hare, the sum of twelve
pounds was paid by the doctors. Their next
victims were an old woman and her grandson,
a dumb boy, and it is recorded that when in
prison Burke confessed that the taking of the
lives of the widow and the dumb boy lay more
heavily upon his heart than all his other acts.

The succession of victims now became
constant and rapid, and in their further quest
for ' subjects ' their most daring and diabolical
exploit lay in decoying to Log's lodging-house,
in September 1828, James Wilson, the bare-
footed and bare-headed imbecile known to
every inhabitant of Edinburgh as ' Daft Jamie.'
Lured to Tanner's Close by Mrs Hare, with
the assurance that his mother was waiting for
him there, ' Jamie,' the universal favourite,
was supplied with drink, and was persuaded
later on to lie down on a bed.

Burke's opportunity had now arrived, and,
throwing himself upon the sleeping simpleton,
he clutched him by the throat and attempted
to strangle him. The attack aroused ' Daft
Jamie,' who seemed to realise the purpose of
the murderer. Grappling with his assailant,
he threw him off, and, springing to the floor,
awaited another onset. Burke again seized

the imbecile, but 'Jamie' had the greater strength, and was overpowering Burke, when Hare caught him by the heels. Even then it took the monsters all their time to accomplish the ghoulish task of holding his nose and mouth until their victim was lifeless. That very night the body was put into a box, and taken to Surgeon's Square, and the usual sum quickly handed over. The disappearance of 'Daft Jamie' from the streets of Edinburgh was much commented upon at the time; and it seems strange that although, as was afterwards found out, Dr Knox and the students recognised the body when on the dissecting table, the horrible crimes were not brought at this point to light.

Not long afterwards there also disappeared from the streets of Edinburgh a handsome girl known as 'Bonnie Mary Paterson'; but it was only at the trial that the public learned that she had been done to death by Burke, in the house of his brother in Gibb's Close, in the Canongate.

At length the long train of crimes was brought to a close. The discovery of a body in the house of Burke, by a man named Gray, immediately led to the arrest of the participants in the crimes. A bribe of ten pounds a week was offered by Helen M'Dougal, but, fortun-

ately for human lives, Gray declined the offer
and informed the police.

The trial of William Burke and Helen
M'Dougal, in the Justiciary Court, on the
24th of December 1828, caused a feverish
excitement over the whole of the country.
There were fifty-five witnesses for the prosecu-
tion, including Hare and Mrs Log, who had
turned King's evidence, and the Lord Advocate had little difficulty in proving the guilt
of Burke, who was sentenced to death by Lord
Boyle, the presiding Judge. The charge
against Helen M'Dougal, however, was found
'not proven.'

Resigned to his fate—for Burke knew there
was no hope of a reprieve—at four o'clock
on the morning of the 27th of January 1829
the condemned man was removed from the
Calton to the lock-up. All that day the din of
the workmen and the clang of the hammers,
mingled with the joyous shouts of the people
who had turned out in thousands to watch the
erection of the gibbet, could be distinctly
heard in the cell where Burke was confined.
At seven next morning Burke was aroused
from his sleep and conveyed to the head of
Libberton's Wynd. The magistrates, dressed
in their robes and with their rods of office,
were waiting, and Williams, the hangman,

speedily adjusted the noose. Breathless silence held the multitude, which extended from the Bowhead to the Tron Kirk. The white-cotton nightcap was drawn over the distorted face, and the next moment a fiend in human guise was launched into eternity. Amidst the deafening yells of exultation from twenty thousand voices, William Burke had justly paid the penalty of his crimes.

On the fate of the other conspirators in the Tanner's Close tragedies it is unnecessary to dwell, except to say that Hare shortly afterwards had a miraculous escape from a burning limekiln in England, into which he had been thrown by infuriated workmen who had discovered his identity. Now blind, and hunted from place to place, he ultimately died in a miserable cellar in the East End of London, crying in his agony, ' I've taken many lives, but I haven't the courage to take my own !'

Thus the curtain was rung down on one of the darkest episodes in the whole of Edinburgh's history.

CRIPPLES' DAY.

IT has been said, and truly, that one half of the world does not know how the other half lives.

Edinburgh, unfortunately, is no exception to the rule. In spite of its historic associations, noble thoroughfares, and rural retreats, one has only to spend a day at Ratho with the participants in the *Courant* trips to realise the difficult problem that confronts the willing workers on behalf of Auld Reekie's poor bairns.

It was my good fortune to be present at a recent cripples' outing—an outing, thanks to the generosity of the Edinburgh High Constables, that could not fail to leave an indelible impression on those who accompanied the children to the country for a day. The activities of the High Constables in connection with city functions are too well known to require recapitulation, but no work carried through gives more genuine pleasure to that old and honoured body than the services rendered by them on Cripples' Day.

It was a happy thought that inspired the Moderator and those associated with him to subscribe a yearly sum sufficient to cover all the costs of taking over six hundred bairns to one of the beauty-spots of Greater Edinburgh. From east, west, north and south they came, including Leith and Portobello, under the guidance of sympathetic teachers from the various schools. And what a sight of smiling, expectant faces!

As I sat in a railway carriage, packed like herrings in a barrel, with a wee Maggie on my knee, a deafening cheer broke from hundreds of lusty throats, indicating that the train had taken its departure. And what shouts of glee when it entered a tunnel! Like larks in their freedom flying through the air, budding Carusos and Pattis gave vent to their overjoyed feelings in snatches of popular songs—some with a dreamy waltz refrain, others of a martial spirit, like 'The March of the Cameron Men!'

During the short journey nothing seemed to escape their attention. 'There's Princes Street Gairdens!' shouted an eight-year-old from Panmure Close, and the others clapped their hands with glee. 'Mister, is there no' ony heather?' was one of the questions put. Green fields and grazing sheep were great attractions to those bairns released from the slums. On the train's arrival at Ratho willing workers were ready to attend to the 'guests.' The field was within a stone-throw, but many had to be carried—cripples from birth, others legless, delicate, and mentally deficient. What a sight to the beholder as they were helped up the brae, and reached

the ground with their 'tinnies' and mugs!
Swings were immediately commandeered,
skipping-ropes set agoing, wickets pitched,
and football started.

Panmure Close.

When lunch-time arrived, hungry stomachs
did full justice to the pies and milk. Many
of the bairns looked healthy and well-cared
for; others, thin and sickly, sent a pang

through the heart. And what makeshifts at respectability! There was Wee Peter, with the holes in his jacket darned with worsted; while Johnnie, who, until the day previous to the trip was bootless, now, by the kindness of his teacher, sported new socks and a second-hand pair of shoes, a couple of sizes too big— but that little mattered! Tommy's mother's ingenuity enabled her to send her faitherless laddie to Ratho likewise. 'His jaicket was a' holes,' as she apologetically explained before the train started, 'and I didna want Tammy to miss the trip, so I washed oor Jeannie's jersey, and see hoo braw he looks in it!' Tears were in the war-widow's eyes as she spoke. Tommy not only looked 'braw in his sister's claes,' but felt justifiably proud!

Then the sports began, and whether the runners could 'sprint' or not and break the tape, there was a prize for everyone. Thoughtful High Constables! And so the day passed all too quickly, with afternoon tea. The dark clouds overhead had passed away, and the sun shone forth as if smiling on the bairns. Then homeward bound—back to their drab surroundings—the squalor and dirt of the city slums!

It is a far cry from the days when, along with other boys, I used to pull the ropes of the old High Street fire-engine, as it lumbered on its way to many a fire. The engine was housed at the head of Fleshmarket Close, and in a flat above were the publishing-offices of

The Canongate.

the *Edinburgh Courant*. There I first made the acquaintance of the late Mr Anderson, through whose instigation the *Courant* trips were founded in 1883.

I can still remember his enthusiasm for the

welfare of the 'mitherless bairns' of the Royal
Mile, and how his eyes would become dim
with tears as he related some touching episode
that had come under his notice. No one at
that time knew more of the degrading environment and awful conditions of those forced to
live in the dark and foul-smelling wynds and
closes of the High Street.

Mr Anderson's work has borne good fruit,
and it is being worthily carried on by willing
workers. Trades Holiday week in Edinburgh
is a busy time for the directors of the *Courant*
Fund trips. There are four days' outings,
and six thousand children enjoy a day in
the country. To many it is the only happy
one away from their squalid surroundings in
the three hundred and sixty-five; so 'Dinna
forget the bairns.'

FAMOUS OLD CIRCUSES.

I AM tempted to revive some memories
of circuses half a century ago, although
the sawdust ring does not appeal to the
public as it used to do. It is a far cry to the
days when penny-gaffs, the diorama, and a
circus were established in the Lothian Road.
They occupied the vacant ground where
the Caledonian Railway Goods Station now

stands, and were eventually swept away to make room for a much-needed improvement. I still remember the canvas erection, and the joy that was felt as the bare-backed horses sped round the ring, the fair damsel in spangles performing various difficult evolutions to the rhythm of the band. The performance finished with a spectacular pantomime, 'Cinderella,' with dozens of children singing 'Cheer, Boys, Cheer!'

Recalling his early days, Robert Louis Stevenson in 1881 confessed to me that while on his way from the West End to Swanston he occasionally visited the shows in Lothian Road, and enjoyed the fun.

All of us have had a first little love affair. My first sweetheart was the young lady with the long-flowing golden hair and spangled dress, who captivated the hearts of the laddies visiting the circus. I have to confess it was a case of love at first sight, followed by a severe attack of sleeplessness for over a week. Three nights in succession I visited the canvas erection, enamoured and spell-bound with her daring performance on the flying trapeze. Surreptitiously, on the Saturday night, when the entertainment was over, I made my way to the artistes' exit, to await the appearance of my 'charming

divinity.' Almost needless to say, disillusion-
ment quickly followed. Accompanied by
her husband, my 'sweetheart' stepped out
of the tent, and I followed them to their
lodging in Boak's land, West Port, a sadder
and wiser boy. The little lady of my dreams,
divested of her alluring spangled garments
and powder and paint, was more than 'sweet
seventeen'!

We read much in the Press nowadays
about the schemes of Councillors in connection
with new and arterial roads to help the unemployed, but I make bold to say that few
of the citizens of Auld Reekie are acquainted
with the history of Lothian Road. Much
has been made of the central poles, and the
conversion from the cable to the electric
tramway system in Princes Street in one
night: but in 1784 our forefathers did a bit
of work that puts this present-day 'hustle'
entirely in the shade.

Before the Lothian Road was formed, a
roadway from the west end of Princes Street
to run southward towards Bruntsfield Links
had long been projected, but many objections
were raised by proprietors of barns, byres, and
sheds which stood in the way. An officer of
the Royal Navy, Sir John Clerk, Bart., of
Penicuik, however, laid a bet with a friend,

that he would, 'between sunrise and sunset, make a road, extending nearly a mile in length, by twenty paces in breadth.'

It happened to be the winter season, when many men were unemployed. He had no difficulty in collecting several hundreds of these at the Kirkbraehead upon the appointed morning before sunrise, when he gave them all a plentiful breakfast of porter, whisky, and bread and cheese, after which he ordered them to set to work: some to tear down enclosures, others to unroof and demolish cottages, and a considerable portion to bring earth wherewith to fill up the natural hollow to the required height.

The inhabitants, dismayed at so vast a force and so summary a mode of procedure, made no resistance; and so active were the workmen that before sunset the new Lothian Road was sufficiently formed to allow the bettor to drive his carriage triumphantly over it, which he did amidst the acclamations of a great multitude of persons, who flocked from the town to witness the issue of this extraordinary undertaking!

At one time a circus and menagerie stood at the head of Greenside Row; and there may be a few alive who remember Newsome's Circus in Broughton. Hengler's then tried

their luck with a wooden erection behind
Brown Square (now Chambers Street), and
a little to the west of the old College Wynd,
where Sir Walter Scott was born. Steep
wooden steps led down to the circus, and at
the entrance ice-cream and hot peas were
sold and nightly relished by many of the
patrons.

Even the old Southminster in Nicolson
Street, where the Empire now stands,
occasionally gave a circus performance.
Henry Powell and Miss Bessie Reid delighted
many 'Soothie' frequenters when they played
'Mazeppa,' with their highly-trained steeds.
At the time of being burned down, the Southminster was in possession of Sam Hague's
Minstrels; and, to recoup Billy Richardson,
the principal of the troupe, and other performers, for the loss they had sustained by
the fire, a successful benefit was held in the
Waverley Market. After being rebuilt, the
Southminster was used as a circus by the
Newsomes. Little Meers, the clown, was a
great favourite with the young folks at that
time, but, although the best of equestrian performers were engaged, the Nicolson Street
circus did not draw the crowd.

Even in those days the Town Council
looked carefully after the interests of Auld

Reekie. Two large pillars and a pair of cast-metal horses were conspicuously displayed at the door of the circus, but, whether as an obstruction or from an amenity point of view, our City Fathers at that time ordered them to be removed. The pillars went to a church, and the two cast-metal horses now decorate the doorway of the west gate of the Corporation Cleansing Department in King's Stables Road—a fit resting-place, surely, for such relics!

Half a century ago the head of Leith Wynd (where Jeffrey Street now stands) was the most favoured spot in the whole city for the boys. Cheap-Jacks, wild Zulus from the Salt-market of Glasgow, Clark's 'Pepper's Ghost,' Harry West's Alhambra, and many other 'attractions' never failed to extract the coppers from their pockets. Swallow's Circus, however, was on a higher plane, and an excellent entertainment was always provided. The proprietor had no reason to be ashamed of such artistes as Chappel and his daughter, who walked the tight-rope. Another performer was Sammy, who created great merriment as he followed the ringmaster round the ring, while that worthy ordered him to 'Ring the bell, Sammy!'—'Yes, papa!' was the plaintive answer. Joe Austin, the bare-backed horse-rider, gave a thrilling performance, but the favourite of those days was, undoubtedly, 'Chee-Ma,' the diminutive clown, who in the ring every night had comical fits from which he was relieved by many drinks from a large bottle. The cure was only brought about by Mr Swallow holding up the empty bottle : then 'Chee-Ma' would rub his stomach and sadly say, 'No more brandy, Mr Swallow? Then no more fits!'

To the present generation possibly the best-known circus proprietor was John Henry Cooke. He came from an honourable line of equestrian performers, and his name will long be remembered in Auld Reekie. A favourite with old and young, rich and poor alike, he did much to raise the tone of his 'shows,' compared with the travelling circuses of his early days. His artistes were always the cream of the 'profession,' and in providing spectacular and novel effects, as far as the limits of a sawdust ring would allow, he had no equal. Of a genial and kind-hearted disposition, his loss is mourned to this day by many he befriended.

A perfect gentleman! The doyen of the sawdust ring! The last time I met 'John Henry,' as he was lovingly called, was near to the door of a well-known howff in the

High Street. He was dressed, as usual, in a tight-fitting braided coat, and wore a tall hat. During our few minutes' conversation we were quickly surrounded by a crowd of his admirers—coalmen, cabmen, chimney-sweepers, and out-of-works. Generous to a degree, his hand, without hesitation, found its way into his pocket. To each he gave a coin with the kindly expression, 'Bless you, my children!' I mildly protested. With a never-to-be-forgotten smile he answered, 'My dear boy, money should be kept in circulation! I feel for the poor!'

Cooke's Circus was established on a vacant piece of ground in Grindlay Street, where the Lyceum Theatre now stands. From there it removed to a substantial brick building in Fountainbridge, now occupied by the Palladium Picture House. Here, at Christmas and New Year time, Cooke's Circus drew crowded houses. My memory goes back to 23rd February 1882, and, as I write, in front of me stands the silver cup I was presented with by good old John Henry Cooke for the best conundrum, in a competition in which there were over three hundred competitors. Competitions in those days were a great draw at the Fountainbridge circus, ponies and pigs also being among the prizes.

Before the advent of music-halls and picture-palaces, circuses were a never-failing source of attraction for old and young, and many grandfathers of to-day, if in a reminiscent mood, may be tempted to tell the bairns around their knees incidents connected with the sawdust ring in the happy auld days noo awa' !

SCOTS COMEDIANS AND THEIR SONGS.

IT is an astonishing fact that, although almost fifty years have passed since the principal 'free-and-easies' in Auld Reekie began to lose their attractions, many of the songs which then became popular are still lilted. Usually, the 'life' of a pantomime or music-hall ditty is about twelve months, a proof that things in the music-hall world are not what they used to be.

This reminds me of the chorus of a song, sung by P. G. Fairley, the Scots comedian, in the old Gaiety in Chambers Street, shortly after that 'house' was opened by Harry Moss:

> I 'm not so young as I used to be,
> When I was a girl of twenty-three ;
> But I 'll maintain, and I 'm not far wrong,
> 'Twas a different world when I was young.

Some people say it is a debatable question whether amusements in general have improved or not. One thing is certain, however: many of the old music-hall songs, with their arresting and alluring choruses, have not been forgotten. If we survey, in a general way, the Scots artistes, who, with their catchy rhymes wedded to simple melodies, enabled the youngsters of Edinburgh to whistle and sing from morning till night, names such as William Crawford, Ben Hoskins, N. C. Bostock, R. S. Pillans, Charles Nicol, P. G. Fairley, Willie Cummings, Tom Maclagan, R. P. Jennings, R. C. M'Gill, and Harry Linn are still remembered.

Here is a typical verse and chorus sung in Harry West's Alhambra:

> In me you see the rale Mackay, without the least
> humbug,
> If ony yin says different, I 'll gie them a daud in the
> lug;
> My subject is legitimate, I 'll have you all to know,
> I 'm here to-night to give you a sight, and introduce
> my show.
> ' Peep-show!   Peep-show!' I cry wherever I go,
> ' England's Queen and others have seen the wonders
> of my show.'

This ditty was very popular in the 'eighties with the High Street and Canongate boys.

Pollock, the singer, appeared on the stage as 'The Peep-Show Man,' with a roughly constructed wooden box slung in front of him. It would have taken much stretch of imagination to appreciate 'the wonders of the show,' for all that could be seen on putting your eyes to the circular bits of magnifying glass in front of the box was a coloured picture of a Spanish bull-fight, or a wreck at sea!

This form of amusement was much in vogue in the streets of Auld Reekie more than half a century ago. The itinerant show-man rarely turned his youthful patrons away. The usual charge was a halfpenny, but, if a boy or a girl were not the lucky possessor of that coin, a farthing was just as acceptable to the showman. When his 'business' was bad, an empty beer bottle was not despised! Those 'Peep - Show' men might well be claimed to be the forerunners of the picture-house, so popular nowadays.

Fifty years ago Scots comedians, as they termed themselves, were undoubtedly first favourites. 'East is east, and West is west,' says Rudyard Kipling, but the tastes of Edin-burgh and Glasgow were similar so far as local talent was concerned. No evening's pro-gramme was considered complete without a

Scots comic. In Glasgow, James Willison,
W. H. Lannigan, and J. C. Macdonald were
great draws in their day, and it is worth
while recalling the fact that these artistes
were indebted to such song-writers as Tom
M'Ausland and John Pettigrew for the success
they achieved. Poor John Pettigrew! I can
well remember my last meeting with this
writer of hundreds of songs surpassingly
popular in their day. He was a chronic
invalid with an incurable bronchitis. His
songs of patriotism stirred fervour in every
audience; his love and humorous ditties
cheered the hearts of thousands, and yet the
author was literally starving day in and day
out. What a tragedy in life!

J. C. Macdonald's strength as a Scots
comedian lay in his 'patter.' He frequently
appeared at the 'Moss Varieties,' in Chambers
Street, and was also much in demand in connection with trades' soirees held in concert-halls
throughout the principal towns of Scotland.
As a 'dame' impersonator, he was unequalled
in his day.

Willie Cummings was another Scots
comedian who relied more on the cleverness of his 'patter' than on his vocalisation.
This is the sort of stuff that tickled music-hall
and 'free-and-easy' audiences half a century

ago. Of course, the humour of the 'patter' depended entirely on how it was delivered. The comedian had bought an old and worn-out horse in the Grassmarket. On his way home he stopped at the Lawnmarket recruiting-rendezvous to have a refreshment, asking a boy to watch the animal for a minute. Willie had scarcely time to finish his dram when the urchin excitedly appeared at the public-house door. 'Maister!' he shouted, 'yer horse has fa'n doon!'—'Fa'n doon!' gasped Willie. 'Ye stupid wee rascal, ye've been leanin' up against it!'

If my memory serves me right, R. S. Pillans, without whom no Theatre Royal pantomime would have been complete, never appeared at the old Gaiety. His style of 'dame,' always free from the least suspicion of vulgarity, was a character-study some of the latter-day Scots comedians might have emulated with profit. The topical songs of Pillans were always the tit-bits of the panto-mime. In these he scored heavily both at the Royal and the New Edinburgh Theatre, now occupied by the Synod Hall.

I can still vividly recall my first meeting with this well-known comedian. When in my teens Pillans had heard that I possessed the rhyming faculty, and, being anxious to

obtain some additional verses for his topical
pantomime song, 'Oor Auld Reekie,' he found
me at 'The Box,' at Bristo, opposite Greyfriars Bobby. At that time this little news-
paper shop was run by William Kay, Bank
Street, a typical Scot, and one of the most
respected traders in Edinburgh. Pillans
quickly explained the object of his visit, and
in a business-like manner stated the sum he
was prepared to pay. Half-a-crown was the
figure, and, as siller was siller to a boy in those
dear auld days, I undertook the contract!
The verses were written, and amused Theatre
Royal patrons during the run of the pantomime. Working this transaction out later on,
I realised that I had been paid the magnificent
remuneration of a halfpenny a line!

In their own day these Scots comedians
had thousands of admirers, but it must
be confessed that in their impersonations
they lacked the artistry of Neil Kenyon and
Sir Harry Lauder.

A SUNDAY 'FREE CHARLIE.'

ON a nirly morning in January, following
the outbreak of the war, with fleecy
snow falling, and in a disguise that would
have baffled a Sherlock Holmes, I turned in

the direction of the Forrest Road Drill Hall.
At that hour the majority of the citizens of
Edinburgh were snugly in bed. To my
surprise I was informed by a Scots sentry on
guard at the door that the spacious Drill
Hall was occupied by the 'boys,' and that
Edinburgh's 'Free Charlie,' since the outbreak
of the war, had been transferred to the Naval
and Military Institute, 'doon in the Coogate.'

With hawk-like eye the Tommy scrutinised
my dilapidated condition, and the thought
flashed through my mind that he was suspect-
ing me as being a bit of a slacker. Luckily
the grey hairs protruding from my greasy cap
and the furrows of time on my cheeks relieved
my conscience, and seemed to convince the
sentry that the pitiful specimen of humanity
before him was over the military age.

'It's a peety ye're ower auld for the sodgers,'
he ventured to remark. And then, after a
thoughtful pause, 'Onyway, ye'd be sure o'
gettin' yer grub! It's nae joke bein' on tramp
in weather like this. Here's tippence—it's
a' I've got; it'll help to get ye a packet o'
fags!'

To Tommy's dismay I refused the kindly
offer with profuse thanks, and turned my
footsteps in the direction of the Candlemaker
Row. In the early morning gloom the

memorial to 'Greyfriars Bobby,' in its mantle
of snow, stood out in bold relief like a thing
of white marble ; and, as I moved down the
silent brae, a glimpse of the monuments in the
old kirkyard on the left awakened memories
of the past and its martyred men.

Reaching the Cowgatehead, I found that
the streets were no longer deserted. Poorly-
clad men and women from the Grassmarket
'models' and adjacent squalid wynds and
closes, shivering in their rags, were hurrying down the Cowgate. Closely following,
in a few minutes I reached the Naval and
Military Institute. At the entrance stood a
man with a smile of welcome on his face—
a striking contrast to the solemn stiffness of
the proverbial elder at the door. There was
no plate, but instead a large hamper full of
enamelled mugs. One was graciously handed
to me, along with a copy of the *Monthly
Visitor*.

Following the crowd that was trooping in,
I took my seat beside a one-legged, unshaven
young man. The kirk—for until the outbreak of the war the building had long been
well known as the Cowgate Church—was
warm and comfortable. It still wanted a
quarter to eight, but the seats in the body of
the hall were already filled by men, and many

more were coming in. They were mostly of
the same uninviting type of mortals, and still
shivering in their rags, for the condition of
things out-of-doors that morning was difficult
to overcome. The gallery, which had been
reserved for the women-folk, was only half-
filled, and the noise of their wagging tongues
seemed a source of annoyance to the men
seated below, where silence reigned supreme.

From a raised platform the late Dr Maxwell
Williamson, who was a hustling director of
the Free Breakfast Mission, surveyed the
motley crowd; while 'the man at the piano'
played a sacred tune as the choir of lady
singers arranged themselves in front. Everything was being conducted in a quick and
methodical manner. Sankey's book of 'Sacred
Songs and Solos' had been given out, and in
a stentorian voice the doctor announced the
opening hymn:

> Would you be free from your burden of sin?
>> There's power in the blood, there's power in
>> the blood;
> Would you o'er evil a victory win?
>> There's wonderful power in the blood.

The Lord's Prayer, with an audible repetition by the audience, followed. It was an
impressive sight to see the bowed heads of the

bald and grizzly-bearded men—there were few young ones there that morning, for nowhere more than in slum-land had the call for King and Country been patriotically responded to. The 'boss,' as my neighbour familiarly designated Dr Maxwell Williamson, had now left the platform, and presently bags, containing two slices of thickly-cut wholesome bread, with corned-beef, were handed round by a band of willing helpers. This was followed by a liberal supply of steaming tea that the most fastidious could not have found fault with. Even the scarcity of sugar was not apparent that morning at the Edinburgh 'Free Charlie.' During the consumption of the breakfast appropriate hymns were rendered by the choir, and my one-legged companion, whose appetite proved to be much healthier than my own, having quickly finished his meal, wiped his mouth with the back of his grimy hand, and ventured to remark, ' Man, this is great! It's worth comin' oot for a feed like this, even on a cauld mornin'!' I nodded, as if approving of my companion's remark; and after a short pause he again said in a low voice, ''Struth! I could be daein' wi' this every mornin' in the week!'

The breakfast was now finished, and Dr Maxwell Williamson ascended to the plat-

form. Before announcing another hymn, in
language that no one could misunderstand he
cautioned his hearers on the evil of spitting
on the floor. Complaints had been made
regarding the practice, but he was sure that
every man present would loyally support him
in putting a stop to the filthy habit. 'That
is not the kind of impression we wish to
leave behind us every Sunday morning.' A
murmur of approval indicated that the forcibly-
expressed reminder was only needed to enlist
the support of Dr Williamson's 'bairns.'
A short address by the Rev. Dr M'Kenzie
followed. Old veterans and 'Weary Willies'
were visibly moved by the homely exhortation.

Leaving the Institute, the crowd hurried
away east and west—back to the 'models'
and the miserable one-roomed dwellings they
called their homes. Southward bound, I
beheld a man in front whom I recognised as
one of the visitors to the 'Free Charlie' that
morning. He held the familiar 'poke' in his
hand, and as he hirpled along he kept tossing
pieces of bread into the middle of the street.
I was quickly by his side, and mildly remon-
strated. He halted for a moment, and eyed
me keenly ere he spoke. 'It's weel eneuch
for you, but I had sic a fill-up last nicht that
I've nae appetite this mornin',' he explained,

while his face showed the extent of the previous
night's dissipation.   Until the Potterrow was
reached he remained thoughtful ; then he broke
the silence : 'God kens, it looks bad tae
chuck awa' the breid sae kindly gi'en ye, but
I'm thinkin' it's no' wasted—it'll feed the
puir hungry sparrows !'

The thoughtlessness of this one man did
not wholly mar the effect of the scene I had
just witnessed in the Cowgate 'Free Charlie.'
Undoubtedly, the flotsam and jetsam of
humanity were thankful that morning for the
mercies received in such pleasant surroundings, and the Scriptural texts were forcibly
recalled—'Though I have all faith, so that
I could remove mountains, and have not
charity, I am as nothing. . . . Charity never
faileth.'   Truly, in the Cowgate 'Free Charlie'
abide 'faith, hope, charity, these three ; but
the greatest of these is charity.'

It is gratifying to know that the Edinburgh
Free Breakfast Mission is still being carried
on at the People's Palace in the Cowgate.
Two of the stalwarts, Mr Robert Wilson and
Dr Maxwell Williamson, have passed away,
but others who have been associated with
the object almost from the beginning—Mr
J. Farmer Brown, Mr Christopher Cairns, and
Mr Hunter Brown—are still labouring there

for the betterment of 'the bottom dog.' All honour to these men whose untiring zeal for the human 'derelicts' of Edinburgh is little known, but whose good work is its own reward.

AUCTION SALE-ROOMS.

LONG before the days when I read 'Quinneys' I must confess that I had a sneaking regard for anything antique. Watching the auctioneers' advertisements in the Press was part of my daily existence, and the red flag waving in the east-endy west-endy breeze, or hanging limply to the gate of some ticketed 'house to let,' was as attractive as the proverbial bull-story. Luckily for my 'bawbees,' the auction-sale fever has worn off to a great extent, and only occasionally am I tempted to join the eager throng. Many educative and profitable hours, nevertheless, have been spent at auction sales; and, looking at the art treasures on the walls or the rare first editions in the bookcases of my 'den,' I am reminded of exciting times ere I carried off triumphantly the object of my heart's desire.

Auld Reekie's house-furniture sales can claim to meet the wants of the rich as well as the poor. A sale at the Market Cross, in the

High Street, by 'warrant of the Court,' always
draws a motley crowd of brokers from the
Cowgate and West Port, along with poor but
aspiring 'guidwives frae the wynds and closes,'
who, with a shilling or two in their pouch,
have resolved to give the guidman a happy
surprise.   Surprise!   Shock would more
appropriately describe the effect when at night
the lord and master views with disgust the
purchase of the day. 'Half-a-croon for that
teapat?' he says with sullen face. 'Ye're
a fule, Meg, to spend yer siller on siccan-like
trash.' 'But it's German silver!' answers his
wife proudly. 'I was telt it was valuable by
a broker, because there's what he ca'd a
mon-on-ogram cut oot on the side o't!'
'Havers, Meg!' retorts John; 'it's leed, and
there's as muckle verdigris inside o't as
wad pushion the haill o' the folk on the stair.'

War-time was the means of putting into
circulation many 'tall stories' concerning the
thriftlessness of the people; and, although there
may have been some truth in the statements,
the charges brought against soldiers' wives
regarding their extravagant propensities at
that time are like the 'war-babies' outcry—a
bit of a myth. We were told that musquash
coats bedecked from head to foot the once
ill-clad factory lassie; and that the munition-

worker's wife, living in many of the tumble-
down tenements in the auld toon, aping the
West End ladies as they sauntered along the
spacious Princes Street pavement on a Sunday
afternoon or evening was a sight for the gods!
Such statements must be taken with the
proverbial 'grain of salt'; and, if those of the
humbler order came into 'a little of their
own,' who could begrudge them what, we
fear, was only a short-lived pleasure?

A run on second-hand pianos and old sideboards, too, sent the prices up with a bang,
and here, again, that lying jade Rumour had
it that soldiers' and munition-workers' wives
were the cause of the inflated prices at Edinburgh auction-sales.

Time was when a square piano or an early-
Victorian sideboard could be had for an old
song. Now, it has to be admitted, things
have changed, and those with furniture to
sell are undoubtedly having the opportunity
of their lives. The charge that was made
against soldiers' wives as to the buying of
pianos, to be 'upsides with their betters,' was
devoid of truth. The real cause—and I have
it on the authority of those in the trade—is
that, owing to the shortage of skilled labour,
dealers with an eye to business were looking
well ahead. Much of the good old stuff had

been bought for the express purpose of being
shipped to America, where the cute Yankees
had been piling up the dollars through the
war, and were anxious to imitate the canny
Scots, with their pianos, substantial sideboards,
grandfather clocks, and lug easy-chairs!

What memories must be recalled at many
a sale of household furniture by those who, in
the 'palmy days' of its possessors, enjoyed
their afternoon 'at home,' or dined in the
evening at the hospitable board! The house,
until recently the pride and joy of its mistress,
is ruthlessly invaded by rich and poor. The
rooms, once so sacred and peaceful, are
crowded with a garrulous, perspiring lot of
human beings, panting for 'just a little fresh
air!' Brokers and bargain-hunters are seldom
addicted to qualms of conscience. Family
heirlooms from the smallest and cheapest
nick-nacks are examined and criticised without the slightest respect for the old associations of their late owners. From the cooking
utensils in the kitchen to the lumber in the
attics, nothing is sacred to the gaze of the
amateur bargain-hunters, the brokers, and the
lady who drives up in her motor-car. In-
expensive memorials of childhood's days, such
as school-books, water-colour sketches, and
toys, now lying in a corner, are sold for a

sixpence—'rubbish' which, years hence, affection would gladly repurchase at its weight in gold, if that were possible.

It is the dining-room and the drawing-room, however, that attract the 'Quinneys' of the trade, with an occasional bride-about-to-be, who is usually accompanied by her happy ma; for, to parody Tennnyson's lines, 'In the spring the young folks' fancy turns, not to thoughts of love, but to—auction-sales!' The affable auctioneer has mounted the chair, and, assured that his clerk and John the handyman are quite ready, his hawk-like eyes at a glance professionally 'measure' the crowd. New customers are there, as well as the 'old familiar faces' of men and women whose bargain-hunting mania, week in and week out from January to December, never seems to wane. Anything they consider cheap is bid for without the least hesitation, but I have often wondered if the game is worth the candle. Many of the sale devotees, after reaching home and having time to examine the 'bargains' carefully, must often be not only sadder but wiser women and men. As for the auctioneers, they are not to blame. They follow not only a legitimate but an honoured calling. The truth is, many are so obsessed with the bidding fever that they

dearly pay for almost every lot they buy.
Hundreds of houses must be stored with
incomplete sets of china, broken fenders,
musty stuffed birds, ancient-looking cradles,
mutilated coal-scuttles, and all kinds of
trumpery whose proper place would be the
scrap-heap of forgotten things.

For more than a couple of hours, prefaced
with a running fire of jocular comments that
tickles the fancy of the smirking dames and
is thoroughly enjoyed by the men, the
auctioneer has been 'doing his bit' to wile
the bawbees from the purses and pockets
of those present.

'Remember, ladies, this is not the old time,
and everything's up in price,' is the sweet-
smiling reminder. 'Here is a table, massive
and antique. Who will say a couple of
pounds to start it? Why, ladies, the varnish
on it is worth more than double!' Two
pounds is quickly offered, and the bids rise
to three guineas. 'Why, bless me, that didn't
pay for the making of the legs!' Eventually
the article fetches five pounds.

'An excellent piano, ladies,' says the
auctioneer. 'Like golf, it's a thing you're
never too old to learn. Fit for cottage or
mansion, as sound as a drum, and guaranteed
to play anything you like. It's German-

make, and worth fifty pounds. I'll start it at ten.' 'Guineas!' says a nervous voice. 'I'm offered ten guineas,' says the auctioneer, with a look of disappointment. 'Why, this is worse than giving it away for nothing! Surely you haven't looked at the article. It will bear inspection. It's worth three times the offer.' 'Eleven pounds,' ventures the trembling Mrs Tamson. 'Eleven-ten,' says a broker. 'Eleven-fifteen!' cries the now excited Mrs Tamson, and ere another bid is made the piano is hers. At the drawing-room door one of the purchaser's neighbours whispers to her companions, 'Fancy that, noo, the wumman's daft! Mistress Tamson wi' a piano! Sic extravagance in thae hard-up times. Wiser-like if she'd cleed her bairns!' 'I hae an inklin' o' what she's efter,' whispers the woman's companion. 'She'll be gaun to tak' in gentlemen lodgers!' sneers the other. 'Set her up wi' gentry airs! A hantle sicht better if she'd pay her last hauf-year's rent!'

The 'lane' sales, where an almost inde-scribable collection of articles are disposed of behind the auctioneer's premises, are a favourite rendezvous of the poorer brokers and buyers. Here often a bit of luck falls to the dealer. Picked up for a few shillings, after a day or two's 'faking' by an expert at the

work, the renovated 'find' can easily bring as
many pounds. Failing a quick sale in the
dealer's shop, the furniture is often returned
to the same auctioneer for sale, and, sand-
wiched between a few choice bits in the
spacious saloon, it finds a ready purchaser, and
a handsome profit is made. This is one of
the tricks of the trade, and it is difficult for
the tyro to discover how he has been done
after the decayed cabinet-maker and the
French polisher have tackled the job.

The buying of antiques is a craze with some
people and a business with others. Budding
'Quinneys' usually know the genuine from
the 'fakes.' A choice bit of the right stuff,
such as Cromwellian, Queen Anne, or Jaco-
bean, gladdens their hearts. Credit must be
given the 'trade' for their love of the old.
Environment may have something to do with
their enthusiasm, but it has to be confessed
that many of the dealers, when they pick
up a treasure, simply look at the article,
no matter what its history may be, from a
business point of view.

The moralist may often wonder why so
many non-buyers daily waste their time at
Edinburgh house-furniture sales. Like the
Sphinx, it still remains a mystery. From
time immemorial the craze has continued to

the present day, and proves as attractive to women as the popular 'movies,' and as exciting to men as a New Year handicap at Powderhall, or a football match at Tynecastle.

JOCK: A WAR-TIME HERO.

UNDER a sweltering August sun I left the Braid Hills car at the terminus, and, leisurely ascending, reached Fairmilehead. Halting for a minute, I turned in the direction of 'Modern Athens,' and my pulses throbbed with pride as I gazed on a vision of matchless beauty—'the quaint, gray-castled city where the bells clash of a Sunday, and the wind squalls, and the salt showers fly and beat.' This description, however, ill fitted Auld Reekie that afternoon. Before me, in all its queenly and romantic grandeur, lay the city, bathed in a dazzling splendour of shimmering gold.

Continuing my journey, I reached the narrow road—'the mile and a bittock' that led to Swanston. In a field near-by sat a solitary figure, like that of a tattie-bogle set up to scare away the crows. I spoke to the man—a bronzed and wounded 'Jock' home from the front, and, like myself, one of the

'R.L.S.' cult, making a hurried pilgrimage to Swanston cottage, 'that little cottage among the hills of home.' Jock, to refresh his memory, had been doing a motor-round that day by Penicuik, West Linton, and the Carlops. 'I gang back to France the morn, and I micht never hae anither chance, so I wasna gaun to miss this ane!' he explained. 'Ay, the Carlops is grand for the likes o' me that's been through hell,' he continued, 'and a sicht o' auld Mrs Veitch at the inn reca'd to my mind mony happy 'oors at Habbie's Howe in my coortin' days.'

Our hero had been 'bookish' before he threw in his lot with 'the contemptible little army,' and what took him to Swanston he quickly explained in garrulous Doric. 'I aye had a liking for Stevenson frae the day I read *Treasure Island*. The speerit o' adventure is in me—that accoonts for me no' being a slacker! This,' he added, pointing to an ugly scar on the cheek, 'I hae as a memento o' the retreat frae Mons! Man, it's only a flea-bite, and it's a guid job I'm mairrit!'

With my brave-hearted hero I trudged along the narrow cart-road that led up to the cottage, his amusing bits of philosophy in Scots making the journey seem easier. Reaching the now famous nook at the foot

of the Pentlands, I recalled to his memory
the wisdom of our City Fathers long ago in
recuperating their jaded senses in such an
ideal spot, after strenuous debates in the stuffy
Council Chamber, and the 'ongauns' that
doubtless took place when old cronies met.
Bareheaded, we gazed at the shaded, immortal
cottage, 'a little quaint place of many rough-
cast gables and grey roofs, hidden away in
the trees of the garden,' that for years
sheltered Robert Louis Stevenson, and Jock's
eyes glistened with tears !

We wended our way to Halkerside and the
tiny pool where the future romancer and poet
'loved to sit and make bad verses.' We
cracked, too, about Stevenson as a Scots poet,
and Jock repeated the lines of 'R.L.S.,' so
appropriate to the Great War :

> A periwig'd Lord of London
>   Called on the clans to rise.
> . . . called on all to gather
>   From every scrog and scaur,
> That loved their father's tartan
>   And the ancient game of war.
>
> And down the watery valley
>   And up the windy hill,
> Once more as in the olden,
>   The pipes were sounding shrill,

> Where flew King George's ensign
>   The plaided soldiers went ;
> They drew the sword in Germany,
>   In Flanders pitched their tent.

As an admirer of Stevenson, our hero was pleased to learn that at one time he contemplated writing a romance dealing with one of the most interesting periods of Scottish history.

In the quiet of far-away Samoa, what more natural than that the thoughts of R.L.S. should turn to old Craigmillar Castle, with its romantic history and stirring episodes of a glorious past ? The weaving of a story round the ill-fated Mary Queen of Scots, before the evil days came, on her return from France, would have added to the lustre of the writer's name. An historical romance with a mixture of 'St Ives,' 'The Master of Ballantrae,' and 'Weir of Hermiston' would have increased to thousands the interest in the ancient Craigmillar monument of feudal times. We can imagine the delight of the reader perusing pages peopled with warriors and courtiers of the time of Mary and Bothwell. And how the vivid imagination of Stevenson would have revelled in descriptions of the old ruin, with its massive walls and gateways ; its vaulted hall, mullioned windows, and sculptured arms; its courtyards, tapestried apartments, and all the paraphernalia associated with a royal residence. What a treasure in literature lovers of Scotland have lost!

On the homeward journey Jock became a little less talkative. Doubtless he was thinking of the scenes of his youth and of home-ties—the wife and bairns he would again leave behind next day. 'Man, ye leeve in an earthly paradise here!' he ventured at length as we turned a bend in the road, showing fields of waving yellow corn and furzy hillsides, with the sun glinting through the trees. We parted, at the foot of the brae, but, ere my hero hirpled off, he said, 'If I'm spared, I'll send ye a bit screed frae — somewhaur in France.'

Weeks passed, and the man from Mons had almost slipped from my memory. One morning, however, an envelope was placed in my hand—one familiar to most folk then, and stamped 'Army Post Office—Passed Field Censor.' When I broke the seal, my visit to Swanston was instantly recalled. The letter was from my hero, Jock. In simple language it told how he was again doing his bit for humanity—somewhere in France.

After telling of the 'Great Push,' he enthusiastically wrote: 'I'm prood to be a Scot after what I ha'e seen oot here! The Kilties are worth their weight in gold! I often think aboot Auld Reekie and oor visit to Swanston. The next time ye are up by Fairmilehead, dander a bit farther on, and pu' a bit heather frae aff the Pentlands. There's plenty o' it there, as ye brawly ken. Then, for luck, be sure and send me a wee bit sprig o't.'

Next day the heather was sent off to my hero. A few weeks passed, but no reply came from Jock. Somehow I felt uneasy, for he had faithfully promised to acknowledge the sprig by return. To set my mind at rest, through the darkened streets of Edinburgh I picked my way in search of the humble abode of my hero's wife and bairns. Ascending the stair of one of the tall tenements in a densely populated part of the Pleasance, I knocked at the door, and it was opened by a woman with an infant at her breast. Quickly I explained my errand, and, bursting into tears, she asked me into the room. 'Yesterday,' she said, trying to stifle her emotion, 'I got this letter frae France. It's frae the colonel o' the regiment, tellin' me that—that Jock is deid! He was a guid man to me, and I'll miss him sair!' The woman's sobs broke the silence as I read the letter vividly describing the heroism of Jock on the Somme. 'Scots pluck was never better shown in "No Man's Land" that night,' the colonel, in conclusion, wrote; 'and your husband died a hero in the truest sense of the word!'

With tears in my eyes I turned to a little room where the widow's three bairns soundly slept. Assuredly the memory of that great sacrifice would make them noble men!

THE END.

Edinburgh: Printed by W. & R. Chambers, Limited.

TRADITIONS OF EDINBURGH
By ROBERT CHAMBERS, LL.D.   21s. net.

ILLUSTRATED BY J. RIDDEL, A.R.S.A.

WITH 30 CHARACTERISTIC DRAWINGS IN COLOUR AND 60 CHARMING PEN-AND-INK SKETCHES

THE SPEAKING HOUSE

"When I forget thee, Auld Reekie, may my right hand forget its cunning."
—*R. L. Stevenson.*

"A beautiful edition of a book which can never grow old."—*Evening Standard.*

W. & R. CHAMBERS, Ltd., 38 Soho Sq., London, W.1; and Edinburgh

TRADITIONS OF EDINBURGH
By ROBERT CHAMBERS, LL.D.

POPULAR EDITION, 5s. net.

WITH PEN-AND-INK SKETCHES BY J. RIDDEL, A.R.S.A.

MYLNE'S COURT

W. & R. CHAMBERS, Ltd., 38 Soho Sq., London, W.1; and Edinburgh.

THE STANDARD EDITION OF BURNS

Dr ROBERT CHAMBERS'S
Life and Works of
ROBERT BURNS

REVISED AND PARTIALLY REWRITTEN BY
WILLIAM WALLACE, M.A., LL.D.

In Four Volumes, Crown 8vo, cloth, £2

Illustrated from Original Drawings by
C. MARTIN HARDIE, R.S.A.   R. B. NISBET, R.S.A.
W. D. MACKAY, R.S.A.   G. O. REID, R.S.A.
and GEORGE PIRIE, A.R.S.A.

In this Edition Dr Wallace has spared no trouble to secure and present the true reading of all the poems; to elucidate difficulties by notes and explanations; to give a full marginal glossary of Scots words likely to puzzle the reader; to make the Edition more complete, by the addition of poems, versicles, and songs not included by Dr Chambers; and to incorporate all new biographical and historical facts.

The poems, the biography, and the letters are so combined and arranged as to show their relation to one another, to present a view of contemporary social life in Scotland, and to illustrate the circumstances in which Burns lived his life and wrote his immortal poems.

Respecting such an arrangement, it is interesting to read that Lord Rosebery, in the course of the Address which he delivered at St Andrew's Hall, Glasgow, on the occasion of the Centenary Celebrations, and in which he described Dr Wallace as that "high and excellent authority," expressed himself in the following terms :—

"I must confess myself, then, one of those who think that the life of Burns doubles the interest of his poems. . . . *The life of Burns I love to read with his poems.* . . . It is a life of worth, and truth, and tenderness."

Sir J. M. BARRIE writes—"I have read your estimate of Burns's character and genius with uncommon pleasure. As for the genius, that he is the great poetic glory of Scotland, none, I suppose, would now seek to deny; but as for his character, you seem to me to offer the truest conception of it I have ever read. He was a great soul who had to fight a grim fight with himself all through, and to half win the battle, as you show so elaborately he did, was a great achievement. I remember Stevenson writing to me about some other writer : 'The author may not be like his books—he *is* his books.' And Burns *is* his poems."

W. & R. CHAMBERS, Ltd., 38 Soho Sq., London, W.1; and Edinburgh

6/- net

Poetical Works of Robert Burns

Edited by WILLIAM WALLACE, LL.D.

A BEAUTIFUL EDITION

WITH ILLUSTRATIONS BY W. D. MACKAY, C. MARTIN HARDIE, G. OGILVY REID, R. B. NISBET, AND G. PIRIE

6/- net

An Important Contribution to Burns Literature

The Real Robert Burns

By J. L. HUGHES, LL.D.

Author of

"Dickens as an Educator," &c.

Extract from Author's Foreword:

"To do something to help all men and women to a juster understanding of the real Robert Burns is the aim of the writer. Let us learn, and ever remember, that he was a reverent writer about religion, a clear interpreter of Christ's teaching of democracy and brotherhood, a profound philosopher, and the author of the purest love-songs ever written."

W. & R. CHAMBERS, LIMITED

38 SOHO SQUARE, LONDON, W.1; AND EDINBURGH

741 pages, price 7/6 net

A SCOTS DIALECT DICTIONARY

COMPRISING THE WORDS IN USE FROM
THE LATTER PART OF THE SEVENTEENTH
CENTURY TO THE PRESENT DAY

Compiled by ALEXANDER WARRACK, M.A.

Minister Emeritus of the United Free Church of Scotland at Leswalt

WITH AN INTRODUCTION AND A DIALECT MAP BY

WILLIAM GRANT, M.A.

Lecturer in Phonetics to the Aberdeen Provincial Committee for the Training
of Teachers, and Convener of the Scottish Branch of the English Association

———

All Readers of R. L. Stevenson, J. M. Barrie, J. Laing Waugh,
O. Douglas, Captain Campbell, and other Scottish Writers,
should have this volume at their elbow.

———

W. & R. CHAMBERS, LIMITED
38 SOHO SQUARE, LONDON, W.1; AND EDINBURGH